Uncertain future: The JCPOA and Iran's nuclear and missile programmes

Mark Fitzpatrick,

Michael Elleman and Paulina Izewicz

Uncertain future: The JCPOA and Iran's nuclear and missile programmes

Mark Fitzpatrick,

Michael Elleman and Paulina Izewicz

IISS The International Institute for Strategic Studies

The International Institute for Strategic Studies

Arundel House | 6 Temple Place | London | WC2R 2PG | UK

First published January 2019 by **Routledge**
4 Park Square, Milton Park, Abingdon, Oxon, OX14 4RN

for **The International Institute for Strategic Studies**
Arundel House, 6 Temple Place, London, WC2R 2PG, UK
www.iiss.org

Simultaneously published in the USA and Canada by **Routledge**
52 Vanderbilt Avenue, New York, NY 10017

Routledge is an imprint of Taylor & Francis, an Informa Business

© 2019 The International Institute for Strategic Studies

DIRECTOR-GENERAL AND CHIEF EXECUTIVE Dr John Chipman
EDITOR Dr Nicholas Redman
ASSISTANT EDITOR Sam Stocker
EDITORIAL Alex Goodwin, Jill Lally, Gaynor Roberts
COVER/PRODUCTION John Buck, Kelly Verity
COVER IMAGE: Adobe Stock

The International Institute for Strategic Studies is an independent centre for research, information and debate on the problems of conflict, however caused, that have, or potentially have, an important military content. The Council and Staff of the Institute are international and its membership is drawn from almost 100 countries. The Institute is independent and it alone decides what activities to conduct. It owes no allegiance to any government, any group of governments or any political or other organisation. The IISS stresses rigorous research with a forward-looking policy orientation and places particular emphasis on bringing new perspectives to the strategic debate.

The Institute's publications are designed to meet the needs of a wider audience than its own membership and are available on subscription, by mail order and in good book-shops. Further details at www.iiss.org.

British Library Cataloguing in Publication Data
A catalogue record for this book is available from the British Library

Library of Congress Cataloging in Publication Data

ADELPHI series
ISSN 1944-5571

ADELPHI 466–467
ISBN 978-0-367-19705-6

Contents

CONTRIBUTORS

Mark Fitzpatrick is Associate Fellow at the International Institute for Strategic Studies (IISS). Until the end of 2018, he was Executive Director of IISS–Americas and Director of the Institute's Non-Proliferation and Nuclear Policy programme. Prior to joining the IISS in 2005, he was a career US Foreign Service Officer. He helped to shape and implement US policy on the Iran nuclear issue in several different roles, including as Deputy Assistant Secretary for Non-Proliferation (acting).

Michael Elleman is Senior Fellow for Missile Defence at the IISS and the principal author of the IISS Strategic Dossier *Iran's Ballistic Missile Capabilities: A net assessment*, as well as numerous articles on missile proliferation. He previously worked as a missile expert for weapons-inspection missions in Iraq, and spent two decades as a scientist at Lockheed Martin's Research and Development Laboratory.

Paulina Izewicz is Senior Research Associate at the James Martin Center for Nonproliferation Studies with the Middlebury Institute of International Studies at Monterey. Until spring 2018, she managed programmatic work on sanctions and led a Track 1.5 dialogue with Iran for the IISS. She has also worked as a Research Associate at the Institute for Science and International Security in Washington DC, where she focused on the technical aspects of Iran's nuclear programme.

GLOSSARY

AEOI   Atomic Energy Organization of Iran

E3   France, Germany and the United Kingdom

E3/EU+3   France, Germany, the UK and the European Union High Representative, plus China, Russia and the United States. See also the P5+1

HEU   highly enriched uranium

IAEA   International Atomic Energy Agency

IRGC   Islamic Revolutionary Guard Corps

JCPOA   Joint Comprehensive Plan of Action

LEU   low-enriched uranium

MTCR   Missile Technology Control Regime

NPT   Treaty on the Non-Proliferation of Nuclear Weapons (Non-Proliferation Treaty)

NSG   Nuclear Suppliers Group

PMD   possible military dimension

PWG   Procurement Working Group

P5+1   France, China, Russia, the UK and the US plus Germany. See also the E3/EU+3

UNSCR   United Nations Security Council Resolution

WMD   weapons of mass destruction

INTRODUCTION

Mark Fitzpatrick

Only three and a half years after its adoption, the Joint Comprehensive Plan of Action (JCPOA), which aimed to obstruct Iran's potential pathways to nuclear-weapons development, is in danger of falling apart. The agreement, better known as the Iran nuclear deal, was widely hailed throughout the world when it was agreed on 14 July 2015, following negotiations between Iran on one side, and the five permanent members of the United Nations Security Council (China, France, Russia, the United Kingdom and the United States) and Germany – collectively known as the P5+1 – on the other, with the European Union chairing. Diplomacy had forestalled both an Iranian nuclear weapon and military action against Iran that some saw as the default means of preventing the development of such a weapon.

Acclaim for the diplomatic achievement was not universal, however. In the US, perceptions of the nuclear deal were divided along partisan lines. With a few exceptions, Democrats were elated at what their standard-bearer, President Barack Obama, had been able to accomplish. Republicans, on the other hand, believed the JCPOA made too many concessions to Iran, and that additional pressure on Iran's economy could have achieved stronger constraints. Israel and three Arab foes of Iran – Bahrain, Saudi Arabia and the United Arab Emirates – also disapproved. From their perspective, the deal's legalisation of Iran's nuclear programme was less contentious than the fact that it legitimised Iran as a nation-state, and they feared that Tehran would gain influence and strength across the Middle East.

As the Republican candidate in the 2016 presidential election, Donald Trump made his opposition to the JCPOA a key campaign issue, calling it the 'worst deal ever' and vowing to terminate the agreement if elected. It took Trump 18 months to fulfil this election promise: in part because Iran was honouring its commitments but also because his key advisers recognised that withdrawing from the deal would serve no strategic purpose. As more hawkish advisers took over in early 2018, they encouraged Trump's inclination to overturn his predecessor's signature foreign-policy achievement. On 8 May 2018, Trump ceased waiving sanctions as required under the JCPOA and announced his decision to withdraw from the deal altogether. This left it up to Iran to decide whether to continue to uphold its end of the agreement in exchange for uncertain economic benefits from the remaining parties to the deal – trade and investment that was coming under sharp pressure from an aggressive US extraterritorial sanctions campaign.

Why is Trump so hostile to Iran? The reasons are rooted in recent history. Ever since its foundation in 1979, the Islamic Republic of Iran has been a source of Western apprehension. From a Western perspective, the antagonism started with the takeover of the US embassy by Iranian students in November 1979 and their holding hostage 52 American diplomats for 444 days. The US also blames Iran for its involvement in several terrorist attacks against US citizens, both indirectly as a patron of Hizbullah, which in 1983 carried out a suicide bombing on the US embassy in Beirut, and directly, through complicity in the 1996 Khobar Towers bombing in Saudi Arabia. Iran has also harassed US ships in the Persian Gulf, detained several US citizens on spurious charges, trained and armed militia groups in Iraq that targeted US service members, supplied rockets to Hizbullah that are aimed at Israeli cities and propped up Bashar al-Assad's regime in Syria.

Iran has its own list of grievances against the West, beginning with the coup against Prime Minister Mohammad Mossadegh fomented by UK and US intelligence in 1953. Iran remains bitter about perceived Western acquiescence in Iraq's use of chemical weapons in the 1980–88 Iran–Iraq War, and the shooting down of Iran Air Flight 655 by the guided-missile cruiser USS *Vincennes* in 1988, which killed 290 people (including 254 Iranians). Other points of contention include instances of lethal US naval action against Iranian vessels and facilities, and the United States' 2007 raid on the Iranian Liaison Office in Erbil, Iraq, in which the US detained five Iranian diplomats, two of whom were held for just over ten months.

Mutual animosity over such incidents might not have boiled over if Iran had not challenged vital US national interests by pursuing nuclear-weapons development. Iran has always denied working on nuclear weapons, but the evidence is clear, as detailed in, for example, a report by the International Atomic Energy Agency (IAEA) published in November 2015 and documents unveiled by Israeli Prime Minister Benjamin Netanyahu on 30 April 2018. Iran's nuclear-weapons development and its failure to report various nuclear activities violated its commitments under the Treaty on the Non-Proliferation of Nuclear Weapons, or Non-Proliferation Treaty (NPT) as it is better known. This development work was also seen to pose an existential threat to Israel. While Israel is not a treaty ally of the United States, the two states share strong political, religious and cultural ties. The US cannot sit by when Israel feels threatened.

Iran never produced nuclear weapons – unlike Israel, which may have about 200 warheads – and, as far as is known, never made a decision to undertake such production. In fact, in 2005 Iran publicised a fatwa issued by Supreme Leader Sayyid Ali Khamenei against the production, stockpiling and use of nuclear weapons.[1] The fatwa, which was orally stated and variously recorded, did not prevent weapons-development work or retention of the records thereafter. Keeping the files, which Israeli intelligence removed from a warehouse in Tehran in a daring operation in January 2018,[2] was in keeping with a nuclear hedging strategy. Since the mid-1980s, Iran has developed dual-use nuclear facilities in order to have the capability to produce nuclear weapons, should its security circumstances require a change to Khamenei's fatwa.

Blocked by the US and other Western powers from obtaining dual-use technologies, Iran turned to the black market. Beginning in 1987, a shady network led by Pakistani metallurgist Abdul Qadeer Khan provided Iran with first- and second-generation Pakistani centrifuges and associated technology.[3] Expanding on Khan network contacts, Iran developed a sophisticated nuclear-procurement effort that often evaded Western intelligence and law enforcement.

The development of fissile-material production capabilities was key to Iran's hedging strategy. Nuclear weapons can be made using two kinds of fissile material: highly enriched uranium (HEU) or plutonium. HEU is made by increasing the percentage of the fissile isotope uranium-235 from the 0.7% found in natural uranium ore to a concentration of 80% or higher. Plutonium is produced whenever uranium is irradiated in a reactor, though for use in weapons, the plutonium must be separated from other elements in the reactor through a chemical process called reprocessing.

Iran focused on the enrichment route, which it could justify for its civilian use in producing low-enriched uranium (LEU) fuel for research and power reactors. The NPT does not prohibit enrichment or reprocessing – respectively, 12 and ten countries possess these technologies, albeit mostly for weapons purposes. (Japan's civilian use for both is the example to which Iran points.) In response to US pressure over the years to deny it enrichment, Iran has talked itself into believing that this technology is essential to its national sovereignty and energy independence. Fifteen years ago, few Iranians knew what the word 'enrichment' meant. Today, almost all Iranians insist, as a matter of national pride, that they absolutely need it.

Ballistic missiles are also part of Iran's nuclear hedging strategy, although most of its missiles also have a legitimate non-nuclear purpose. Denied replacement parts for US-built aircraft that the Islamic Republic inherited from the Shah, and having been outgunned by Iraqi missiles during the Iran–Iraq War, Tehran turned to short- and medium-range missiles as its primary means of air defence and deterrence. Iran insists that missiles are integral to its sovereignty, with even more fervour than when discussing enrichment.

The fissile-material production efforts that Iran launched in the mid-1980s inched along for two decades under weak management, in the face of strong US pressure to foreclose procurement of dual-use technology. Around the turn of the century, the programme made a breakthrough, with new leadership and a source of black-market nuclear goods and know-how. In 2001, Iran began construction of an underground industrial-scale enrichment facility at Natanz.

In 2002, an Iranian exile group exposed the Natanz facility and a heavy-water production plant at Arak, apparently fed the information by Israeli intelligence, sparking the now long-running Iranian nuclear crisis. France, Germany and the United Kingdom (the E3) initiated negotiations to persuade Iran to stop its enrichment programme, while the US pushed for sanctions at the United Nations to the same end. Neither effort succeeded. Diplomacy briefly stalled the enrichment programme in 2003 and 2004, but Tehran would never agree to forgo this technology. It responded to additional sanctions by adding more centrifuges to enrich uranium.

Recognising the impotence of the negotiating strategy he had inherited from the George W. Bush administration, Obama in 2013 changed US policy to limit, rather than eliminate, Iran's uranium-enrichment capability. This compromise enabled multilateral negotiations, which had been stalemated for eight years, to progress in earnest. The pressure sanctions were beginning to place on Iran's economy also encouraged Iranian diplomats to seek an accord, but they would not budge on key positions until the US conceded on enrichment.

For many Republican critics, acknowledging that Iran could keep its fissile-material production technology was an unacceptable concession. The fact that Iran already possessed the technology was less relevant to opponents than Obama's concession of legitimising the enrichment. Critics also condemned Obama's agreement to limit the scope of negotiations to the nuclear issue, leaving aside Iran's development of ballistic missiles, regional aggression and internal repression.

In voicing their complaints against the JCPOA, critics looked for additional arguments to buttress their case that the US should void the deal. Partisan opponents, for example, seized upon unfounded accusations – including by some well-respected analysts – that Iran was violating the agreement. Except for two very minor and quickly rectified instances of excess heavy-water storage, this was not the case. Yet although the accusations were easily refuted, a narrative of Iranian deceit in implementing the nuclear accord took hold among Republicans, especially those who had Trump's ear and in 2018 joined his national-security team. This narrative of Iranian deception, along with an impulse for regime change in Iran, formed the foundation for his withdrawal from the deal, as explained in Chapter One.

The International Institute for Strategic Studies (IISS) does not share this view of the JCPOA. Researchers in the Institute's Non-Proliferation and Nuclear Policy (NPNP) programme have long been sceptical of Iran's claims that its nuclear programme was entirely for civilian purposes. We saw sanctions as a legitimate and potentially effective means of changing the cost–benefit analysis behind Iran's nuclear decision-making. When sanctions achieved their immediate objective of helping to bring Iran to the negotiating table, however, we assessed that the agreement reached was beneficial. We have not changed this assessment.

This book is a combined effort by IISS NPNP researchers, led by programme director Mark Fitzpatrick, who wrote the first chapter, drawing on analysis published by the Institute since 2015. The second chapter was written by Research Associate Paulina Izewicz (who has since moved to the James Martin Center for Nonproliferation Studies at the Middlebury Institute of International Studies at Monterey) and draws on a paper she wrote with the financial support of the Canadian Department of Foreign Affairs, Trade and Development.[4] Fitzpatrick and Michael Elleman, IISS Research Fellow for Missile Defence, collaborated on the third chapter on Iran's ballistic-missile programme, an earlier version of which, written with the financial support of the MacArthur Foundation, was published in February 2018.[5]

Chapter One addresses the false claims of Iranian JCPOA violations and other criticisms that have been levied against the accord. The chapter recognises that, like any negotiated agreement, the JCPOA was far from perfect, but notes that until Trump withdrew, it was running smoothly. Withdrawing from it was a grave mistake.

Chapter Two returns to the issue of nuclear black-market trafficking and explores the Procurement Channel: a little-known mechanism established by the JCPOA to counter such activity by providing a legitimate way for Iran to procure nuclear-related goods for its limited programme. In asking whether this mechanism is fit for purpose in curbing Iran's covert procurement of nuclear and dual-use goods, the chapter notes the importance of credible enforcement and, most importantly, the viability of the JCPOA itself.

Chapter Three takes up in detail the issue of Iran's ballistic-missile programme. From a strategic perspective, it was regrettable that Iran, Russia and China insisted on excluding missiles from the negotiations. Ballistic missiles are an essential element of a nuclear-weapons programme, which comprises three elements: sufficient fissile material for a nuclear explosion; the physics package to fashion the weapon; and the means of delivering it. Allowing Iran to develop nuclear-capable missiles while there are only temporary limits on its enrichment programme means Tehran would be well placed to develop a nuclear weapon when the limits expire.

Yet not all of Iran's ballistic missiles are able to carry the bulky devices typical of first-generation nuclear weapons, and fewer of its missiles are designed with a nuclear delivery role in mind. United Nations Security Council Resolution 2231, which was adopted to endorse the JCPOA in July 2015, superseded – and departed from – previous Security Council resolutions on Iran. It proscribed Iranian missiles based on their intent (those 'designed' to carry nuclear weapons) rather than solely on their inherent capability. Chapter Three differentiates among Iranian missiles that are so designed and those that are not.

A question mark hangs over the JCPOA. Given Washington's withdrawal and near declaration of economic war against Iran, we fear that the accord may soon be spoken of in the past tense. If so, it will be the world's loss.

Assessing the JCPOA[1]

Mark Fitzpatrick

Origins of the deal

In autumn 2013, Iran appeared to be on the brink of becoming a nuclear-armed state. It had nearly 20,000 uranium-enrichment centrifuges in place and was installing them at a rate of more than 700 per month. Around 1,000 second-generation centrifuge models that were three times more effective appeared to be ready for operation, and more were being prepared for installation. Iran's stockpile of low-enriched uranium (LEU) was growing at an average rate of 150 kilograms per month, and it had almost enough 20%-enriched uranium hexafluoride for a weapon, if further enriched.[2] The underground enrichment facility at Fordow was being readied to produce more 20% product. Meanwhile, the Arak research reactor was nearing completion, and would potentially soon be able to produce enough weapons-grade plutonium for one or two bombs per year. Iran's verification commitments were limited to ordinary International Atomic Energy Agency (IAEA) safeguards, and Iran refused to accept the standard IAEA provisions requiring declaration of new facilities until they were close to being operational. Meanwhile, Israel was threatening to conduct a military attack to stop Iran's nuclear programme from progressing,[3] like the airstrikes it conducted against Iraq's Osiraq reactor in 1981 and Syria's reactor at al-Kibar in 2007.

By 2013, Western powers had been negotiating with Iran for ten years, attempting to curb a nuclear programme with little economic justification and which many Western strategists saw as a stalking horse for nuclear-weapons development. When France, Germany and the United Kingdom (the E3) negotiated with Iran on their own from 2003–05, they persuaded Iran to suspend part of its uranium-enrichment programme, but they could not convince Iran to forgo enrichment altogether. The so-called 'right to enrichment' was a rigid sticking point.

When hardliner Mahmoud Ahmadinejad was elected president in June 2005, prospects for a comprehensive settlement withered. Shortly after his inauguration that August, Iran rejected a 32-page package proposal by the E3, which had held out the possibility of allowing enrichment after a period of cessation (albeit with no firm commitment to this effect). Ahmadinejad defiantly ordered the resumption of enrichment-related activity.

From 2005–10, the United Nations adopted increasingly sharp sanctions resolutions while Iran steadily increased its enrichment capability. In what might be called a race between centrifuges and sanctions, the centrifuges were winning. Uncompromising positions on both sides meant that negotiations between Iran and the five permanent members of the Security Council plus Germany – usually called the P5+1, although referred to in Europe as the E3+3 (the E3 plus China, Russia and the United States) – and chaired by the European Union were fruitless.

In June 2013, the dynamics changed with the election of Hassan Rouhani, a pragmatist who had campaigned on a pledge to improve Iran's stagnant economy by getting sanctions lifted. It is important to note, however, that earlier that year, Ahmadinejad had authorised secret bilateral talks in Oman with emissaries from US President Barack Obama. These talks also had the approval of Iran's Supreme Leader Sayyid Ali Khamenei.

Negotiations made rapid progress that autumn, once the US dropped its long-standing demand for Iran to cease enrichment activities. It had long been clear that the Iranians would never give up something they considered to be their right under the Non-Proliferation Treaty (NPT).[4] Sanctions played an important role in encouraging Iran to participate meaningfully in negotiations, but it was Washington's compromise of allowing enrichment that persuaded Iran to cap and partially roll back its nuclear programme.

These bilateral talks then widened out to become multilateral. In Geneva, on 24 November 2013, Iran and the E3/EU+3 (now the official acronym) struck an interim deal, the Joint Plan of Action (JPOA), implementation of which began in January 2014. In exchange for a halt on further sanctions and a suspension of sanctions on Iran's petrochemical (but not oil) exports and trade in certain other sectors, Iran agreed to stop expanding its centrifuge numbers, to limit enrichment to 5% and to neutralise its existing 20%-enriched uranium stockpile, as well as to stop working on the Arak reactor. The JPOA also provided for enhanced verification. Iran dropped its long-standing demand for a recognised 'right' to enrichment, as long as some level of enrichment was allowed. Meanwhile, parties undertook to continue negotiations, giving themselves a six-month deadline to produce a final deal.

It took 16 months for the negotiating parties to hammer out the general structure of an agreement. By 2 April 2015, limits on Iran's nuclear programme had largely been agreed, when negotiators meeting in Lausanne, Switzerland, announced that they had reached a framework for a Joint Comprehensive Plan of Action (JCPOA). Iran's enrichment capacity would be rolled back for a specified duration; Fordow would no longer be used for enrichment; the reactor at Arak would be redesigned so it could not produce weapons-grade plutonium; and verification would be further enhanced. In exchange, all UN sanctions resolutions would be terminated. Several more weeks of negotiation – with several missed deadlines – were needed, however, to clarify details on sanctions relief, enrichment roll-back and acceptable research and development on advanced centrifuges.

As the JCPOA negotiations were drawing to a conclusion, Iranian leaders began to draw red lines regarding inspections. In a speech on 9 April, Khamenei said that IAEA inspectors would not be allowed to visit military sites or interview Iranian scientists.[5] Islamic Revolutionary Guard Corps (IRGC) commanders echoed his apparent edict.[6] Iran's then-deputy foreign minister and lead negotiator Abbas Araqchi suggested, however, that 'managed access' to military bases might be possible under the IAEA safeguards Additional Protocol.[7] He knew that this strict verification instrument, which Iran would have to accept under the deal, made no exception for the right of inspectors to seek access to any site where they had reason to believe activity involving nuclear material was taking place. Given that the IAEA had already visited Iranian military bases many times in the past and conducted several interviews of Iranian scientists, Iran could not prohibit them in the future.

Hardliners in the United States drew their own red lines. On 9 March, Republican Senator for Arkansas Tom Cotton wrote a condescending letter to Iranian leaders signed by 46 fellow Republican senators, saying they would consider any nuclear agreement not approved by Congress as 'nothing more than an executive agreement between President Obama and Ayatollah Khamenei'. The letter added ominously that 'the next president could revoke such an executive agreement with the stroke of a pen'.[8] Indeed, this is what happened three years later when Obama's successor, Donald Trump, withdrew from the deal, as detailed below.

With Republicans in control of both houses of Congress, it was clear that Obama could not obtain a positive vote of approval for the deal, much less ratification of it as a treaty, which would have required a two-thirds majority in the Senate. Instead, Democrats worked out an arrangement with Republican Senator Bob Corker, chair of the Senate Committee on Foreign Relations, for congressional review that turned the tables. Under what was called the Iran Nuclear Agreement Review Act (INARA), passed in May 2015, opponents of the deal would need a two-thirds majority for a resolution of disapproval of the deal, otherwise it would become law. When over one-third of senators signed a letter supporting the imminent deal, it became clear there would be no congressional blockage.

The deal

The agreement that was finally reached in Vienna on 14 July 2015 included more Iranian concessions than many observers had expected.[9] It required Iran to eliminate all of its usable 20%-enriched uranium and 98% of its 3.5% LEU, and to limit LEU stockpiles to 300 kg for 15 years. Iran had to remove 14,000 of the 20,000 centrifuges installed at the Natanz plant. They would be kept in storage, giving Iran scope to restore enrichment production to previous levels in case the agreement broke down. (In practice, moving the centrifuges likely impaired their functioning.)

For 15 years, enrichment could continue only with 5,060 inefficient and breakdown-prone first-generation (IR-1) centrifuges and only up to 3.67% (the level needed to fuel most power reactors). During this same period, enrichment would cease at Fordow, although the plant could remain open with 1,044 centrifuges in a non-enrichment function to produce stable isotopes. The calandria (core) of the Arak reactor was to be removed and disabled, and the reactor redesigned, so as to minimise its ability to produce weapons-grade plutonium. Iran agreed not to engage in spent-fuel reprocessing for 15 years. Enrichment-related research and development was limited for eight years, after which it could gradually expand at an agreed schedule, as set out in Annex I to the deal. Iran was not to construct additional heavy-water reactors or accumulate heavy water for 15 years; all excess heavy water was to be made available for export to the international market. Iran was restricted to stockpiling no more than 130 metric tonnes of heavy water ahead of the redesign of the Arak reactor.

The JCPOA established the most intrusive monitoring regime applied by the IAEA anywhere in the world. Under the JCPOA, Iran would provisionally apply the conditions of the IAEA Additional Protocol, which allows the agency to access any site at which it has reason to suspect activity involving fissile material is under way. The Additional Protocol has become the international norm, in force in 133 states to date, but it is not mandatory under the NPT. By JCPOA Transition Day, eight years later, Iran would seek ratification of the Additional Protocol, which would then be implemented in perpetuity.

Going beyond this instrument, the IAEA would monitor Iran's uranium mines and milling plants, centrifuge production and assembly sites, and procurement supply chains for 20–25 years. A dispute-resolution process was also established to resolve disagreements on implementation of IAEA access and other provisions. For example, the Additional Protocol allows a state to arrange managed access – as referred to by Araqchi – for various reasons, including to protect information that is proprietary or commercially sensitive. Managed access means the state can propose an alternative means for the IAEA to meet its verification objectives. The IAEA may accept this proposal, propose another alternative or stick to its original request. A body dominated by Western states (see the discussion of the Joint Commission below) would resolve any disputes.

The deal required most of the economic sanctions imposed due to Iran's nuclear activities to be lifted or suspended once the IAEA had certified that Iran had taken the required steps to reduce its LEU stockpile and to remove centrifuges and the Arak reactor core. Sanctions relief would include the release of approximately US$100 billion of proceeds from oil sales, frozen in non-US bank accounts abroad, although the US Treasury assessed that just over US$50bn would actually be returned to Iran because the rest was tied up in foreign investments.[10]

The seven UN Security Council resolutions that had hitherto placed restrictions on Iran were to be replaced by a new resolution, UNSCR 2231, which allowed for restoration of sanctions by a majority vote of the council without a veto right by any member – the so-called 'sanctions snap-back'. The replacement resolution continued restrictions on conventional arms and missile-related transfers for five and eight years respectively, and endorsed provisions of the JCPOA for monitoring legitimate procurement of nuclear-related goods and equipment consistent with the allowed size and function of the enrichment programme (see Chapter Two).

Common wisdom among Western powers held that Iran could not be trusted without such strong penalties for non-compliance. It was not expected that other parties might not honour their commitments under the deal, so no mechanism was included to deal with the withdrawal of the US in May 2018.

Unlike the NPT, the JCPOA has no withdrawal clause. Although most of the JCPOA's limits on civilian nuclear activities end after a specified period of time, the obligations not to engage in nuclear-weapons-related activities are indefinite, as are the key verification measures of the Additional Protocol and Iran's commitment to exporting all spent fuel, making it unavailable for plutonium-based weapons. Among the ways the deal improves on the Additional Protocol is that maximum time periods are set in paragraph 78 for IAEA access to suspicious undeclared sites: 24 days in the worst case, in which the IAEA is unsatisfied with Iran's answer to its concerns. The normal turnaround period for Iran to respond to an inspection request would be 24 hours. Adding an ultimate limit of 24 days is an improvement to the Additional Protocol, which provides for no such limit on delays. While 24 days might seem too lenient in giving a determined cheater time to remove evidence, the US Department of Energy National Laboratories proved that even very limited quantities of uranium could not be cleaned up in this amount of time.[11]

The JCPOA's limits on civilian nuclear capacity also have no equivalent in the NPT. Their imposition for 15 years, in the case of enrichment and heavy-water reactors, would prevent Iran from being able suddenly and without detection to rush to build nuclear weapons after Termination Day. The IAEA would monitor production of key centrifuge parts for 20 years, and track all uranium oxide for 25 years – until 2036 and 2041, respectively.

The accord accomplished what the Obama administration in particular had set as its key objective: blocking all of Iran's potential paths to a nuclear weapon. This was done by extending to one year the 'breakout' time – how long it would take Iran to produce enough highly enriched uranium (HEU) for a weapon at declared facilities (thereby 'breaking out' of the

NPT)[12] – and by providing for extensive monitoring that would give high confidence of detecting enrichment at undeclared sites. A plutonium route to nuclear weapons was foreclosed by the agreement to replace the core of the Arak reactor with one that cannot produce meaningful quantities of weapons-grade plutonium, and by Iran's willingness to forgo reprocessing.

Early on, the negotiating parties agreed to limit the scope of the talks to the nuclear issue. Other issues of contention – including Iran's support for Hizbullah and other non-state actors across the Middle East, accusations about connections with terrorism, its human-rights abuses, its detention and imprisonment of dual citizens and other foreign nationals on spurious charges, and its antipathy to Israel – were of less priority to the P5+1 than blocking Iran's potential path to nuclear weapons. They judged that adding other issues would hopelessly complicate negotiations that were already complex. In a nod to these other issues, however, a preface to the JCPOA stated the parties' anticipation that 'full implementation of this JCPOA will positively contribute to regional and international peace and security'.[13]

In a compromise by the Western parties, Iran's ballistic-missile programme was also excluded from the talks. This would prove to be a key point of contention for critics of the deal, given the role of missiles as the preferred delivery vehicle for nuclear weapons. Although the Obama administration had wanted to include missile restrictions in the negotiations, this was rejected by China, Iran and Russia.[14] US negotiators justi-fied excluding missiles from the negotiations on grounds that if Iran were blocked from obtaining a nuclear weapon, then the matter of delivery mechanisms would be less important.[15] This issue is explored in depth in Chapter Three.

The JCPOA set a schedule for the execution of the steps set out in the deal.[16] The agreement allowed for 90 days between

Figure 1: **JCPOA implementation plan**

2015

14 July 2015
Finalisation Day

P5+1 and Iran conclude negotiations and reach agreement on JCPOA

20 July 2015

UN Security Council adopts Resolution 2231, endorsing JCPOA and terminating previous resolutions on Iranian nuclear issue

18 October 2015
Adoption Day

JCPOA formally takes effect, and preparations begin for implementation of commitments

2016

16 January 2016
Implementation Day

- IAEA confirms Iran has taken actions specified by JCPOA
- UN, EU and US cease application of various sanctions on Iran

2020

October 2020 or earlier upon IAEA drawing 'broader conclusion'

UN Security Council ban on conventional-arms exports to Iran expires

2023

October 2023 or earlier upon IAEA drawing 'broader conclusion'
Transition Day

- UN ballistic-missile sanctions lifted
- Iran to ratify IAEA safeguards Additional Protocol
- EU to lift various sanctions on Iran
- US to legislate for lifting various sanctions

2024

March 2024

Iran may commence testing for up to 30 advanced centrifuges; may begin manufacturing IR-6 and IR-8 centrifuges

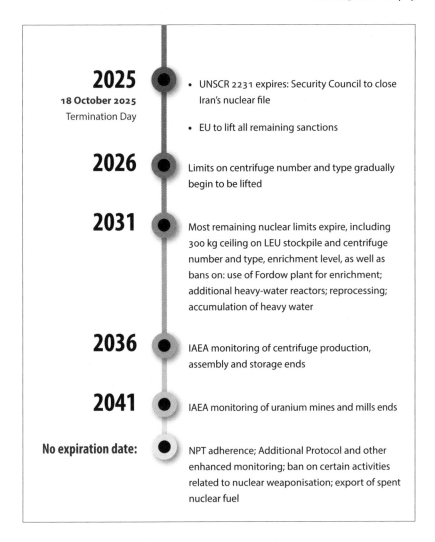

2025

18 October 2025

Termination Day

- UNSCR 2231 expires: Security Council to close Iran's nuclear file

- EU to lift all remaining sanctions

2026

Limits on centrifuge number and type gradually begin to be lifted

2031

Most remaining nuclear limits expire, including 300 kg ceiling on LEU stockpile and centrifuge number and type, enrichment level, as well as bans on: use of Fordow plant for enrichment; additional heavy-water reactors; reprocessing; accumulation of heavy water

2036

IAEA monitoring of centrifuge production, assembly and storage ends

2041

IAEA monitoring of uranium mines and mills ends

No expiration date:

NPT adherence; Additional Protocol and other enhanced monitoring; ban on certain activities related to nuclear weaponisation; export of spent nuclear fuel

the endorsement of the deal by the UN Security Council and JCPOA Adoption Day, at which time the deal would come into effect, allowing time for US congressional review and for Iran to address remaining IAEA questions – in the event, this fell on 18 October 2015. Sanctions relief would begin on Implementation Day, once Iran had met its rollback requirements. This took place on 16 January 2016. EU sanctions regulations and certain other measures would remain in place until Transition Day. This is defined as either eight years after

Adoption Day (i.e., October 2023), or the point at which the IAEA draws the 'broader conclusion' in accordance with the Additional Protocol, 'that all nuclear material in the country remains in peaceful activities, whichever is earlier'.[17] UNSCR 2231 will expire in October 2025 (ten years after Adoption Day, referred to as UNSCR Termination Day in the text of the agreement). At this point, the UN Security Council will close Iran's nuclear file.

Iran's past nuclear-weapons development

In the final weeks of negotiations, how to deal with allegations of Iran's past nuclear-weapons development became a particularly thorny issue. Western parties had no doubts that Iran had conducted such research, as later corroborated by revelations by Israel in April 2018. A controversial US national-intelligence estimate concluded in 2007 that Iran did at one point have a programme to develop nuclear weapons, but had largely suspended this work in autumn 2003, while continuing some aspects of it.[18] The IAEA, which was conducting its own assessment of evidence provided by foreign intelligence agencies, euphemistically called these efforts nuclear activities of a 'possible military dimension' (PMD), a term first used in UNSCR 1929 (2010). IAEA officials were frustrated that Iran had delayed and obstructed the agency's attempts to address alleged past weaponisation work. In November 2011, an IAEA report listed details of 12 kinds of work relevant to weaponisation, for which it had credible information.[19] By June 2015, Iran had partially addressed only one and a half of those allegations, claiming that the activities in question were for civilian purposes and that most of the allegations were based on forged documents.[20]

In accordance with a separate road-map agreement signed with the IAEA in July 2015, Iran was to address by November of that year all of the IAEA's outstanding questions concerning past (and possibly present) nuclear-weapons-related research.[21] Significant sanctions relief under the JCPOA would be dependent on Iran taking all steps specified in the road map.[22] Taking the steps and addressing the IAEA's questions, however, did not necessarily mean that Iran would have to resolve all outstanding issues. The requirement was worded in such a way as to give the IAEA latitude to accept less-than-forthcoming answers.

In accordance with the road map, IAEA Director General Yukiya Amano presented a final report on the matter in early December 2015. It concluded that Iran had been engaged in coordinated research on nuclear weapons and that most of this activity had ceased by 2004; however, some work on computer modelling of a nuclear explosive device continued until 2009, even though these calculations were, in the words of the IAEA, 'incomplete and fragmented'.[23] As US nuclear-policy expert Martin Malin noted, one no longer had to say 'possible' when commenting on the military dimensions of Iran's nuclear programme.[24] The report also expressed confidence that there had been an explosives chamber at the Parchin military base, which Iran had removed along with other traces of nuclear-related work. The report concluded, however, that the nuclear-weapons programme had not advanced 'beyond feasibility and scientific studies, and the acquisition of certain relevant technical competences and capabilities'.[25] The IAEA report said that Iran had addressed all questions (even though it had provided no new information on several issues), but added the caveat that some of Iran's explanations were unconvincing, particularly on the purpose of a certain building of interest at Parchin. The IAEA thus had to leave several matters unresolved, because it was unable to draw firm conclusions. The report, however, indicated that the agency already knew enough about Iran's past activities, and it was not an exoneration. It could be read to say: 'we know what you did, and we know you are lying about it.'

Rather than insisting that the IAEA keep pressing Iran for more answers, the agency's Board of Governors made a political decision on the basis of Amano's report to close the 'military dimension' file. The board judged that if Iran fulfilled its stated obligations under the JCPOA to remove centrifuges, LEU and the core of the Arak reactor, and undertook to apply the Additional Protocol, the benefits would offset the lack of closure on military-dimension issues. Forestalling future weaponisation was judged to be more important than having a full account of the Iranian programme's past activities. In effect, the board gave into a demand by Khamenei, who had said in October 2015 that the closure of the PMD file would be a condition for Iran to remove the core of the Arak reactor and ship out 12,000 kg of LEU.[26] Compromise on this sensitive topic planted the seeds for what would prove to be one of the strongest criticisms of the deal: that Iran had lied about its nuclear-weapons programme, and had not been forced to reveal what it had done.

Criticism and rebuttal

JCPOA opponents typically compare the final agreement to an idealised concept of a better deal – one that would permanently restrain Iran's nuclear programme, with unlimited verification measures, limit its missile programme as well, and, for good measure, compel better behaviour in other policy fields. Better provisions can be imagined, of course, including those that were tabled and eventually traded away in order to persuade Iran to accept the very sharp limits and intrusive verification measures in the JCPOA. Compromise is the essence of negotiations. Along the way, Iran gave up many of its own demands.

According to one Iranian critic, 19 red lines defined by Khamenei were crossed.[27] Critics who insist that renegotiating the deal could achieve far tougher conditions have a wholly unrealistic assessment of Iran's willingness to concede under pressure on points it regards as fundamental to its sovereignty. There is no possibility that Iran would accept nuclear limits in perpetuity that are not required of other states. JCPOA supporters often refer to this ideal as the 'unicorn' arrangement.[28] What follows explores some of the major criticisms of the deal, except for the issue of ballistic-missile development, which is addressed in Chapter Three.

Sunset provisions

The strongest criticism of the JCPOA is levelled at its limited duration: the so-called sunset provision. There had to be some end date to the limits; no sovereign state unless utterly defeated on the battlefield would accept perpetual limits on its civilian nuclear technology. At the start of the negotiations, the US wanted a 25-year limit, while Iran was ready to accept no more than a couple of years. They eventually reached a compromise of ten to 15 years for the key limits on enrichment. This is not a long period, considering that negotiations over Iran's nuclear programme began 15 years ago, over which time there has been no change in its strategic goal of having a nuclear hedging strategy. In the view of many critics, Iran has simply agreed to delay fulfilment of that goal for a relatively short period of time.

While one can legitimately criticise the JCPOA for allowing Iran unlimited expansion of a civilian nuclear programme in 15 years, this hardly paves the way for nuclear weapons, as many critics charge.[29] Rather, it buys 15 or more years of veri-fied non-nuclear status – and the reassurance of not having to resort to war to stop an Iranian nuclear-weapons programme. Iran has strong incentives to honour the deal during this time.

Faithful implementation should give the IAEA the means to be able to draw the 'broader conclusion'. If Iran could earn this IAEA certificate of approval, there would be no sustainable reason not to allow it the same rights enjoyed by other IAEA members such as Germany and Japan, both of which have enrichment programmes.

In an NPR interview on 7 April 2015, Obama stumbled when he appeared to say that Iran's breakout time would shrink to close to zero after as little as 13 years.[30] The State Department spokesperson spun this as saying he meant in the absence of a deal that imposed limits,[31] but critics had a field day. During the period of limits, Iran will be allowed to continue research and development on advanced centrifuges, which it will then be able to use for enrichment after the limits are lifted. Because research and development of those models will be limited to small-sized cascades, Iran would not be able to introduce them in large numbers immediately after limits are lifted. A few years of further development and testing of larger cascades would still be necessary. But after at least 18–20 years, the breakout time would drop to an alarmingly short period of several weeks. If the deal survives that long, years of intrusive IAEA monitoring will go a long way toward demonstrating good faith, based on concrete, empirical evidence. In such a scenario, faithful implementation would enable the IAEA to draw the broader conclusion.

IAEA inspection rights

In early April 2015, towards the end of the JCPOA negotiations, US Deputy National Security Advisor Ben Rhodes told CNN that the agreement would provide for 'anywhere, anytime, 24/7 access as it relates to the nuclear facilities that Iran has'. Energy Secretary Ernest Moniz similarly said in July 2015 that the deal would provide for 'anytime, anywhere' inspections.[32]

Critics of the deal seized upon this exaggerated claim when the actual access rights turned out to be something less.

The 'anytime, anywhere' catchphrase emerged from the case of Iraq, where the regime of Saddam Hussein, after being soundly defeated in the First Gulf War of 1990–91 (*Operation Desert Shield*), had to accept inspection conditions imposed by UNSCR 687. As the result of negotiations, rather than a defeat, Iran's case is dissimilar. Iran has a legitimate need to protect military secrets that are unrelated to illicit nuclear activity. No sovereign state – especially one threatened by airstrikes – would willingly expose its defences.

Although the JCPOA does not provide for 'anytime, anywhere' inspections, it does provide for access as needed to verify that Iran is honouring its commitments. The IAEA can make an expedited inspection request for 'complementary access' to sites about which it has legitimate questions concerning possible nuclear activity or anomalies in host-state reporting. Complementary access is requested in various situations, often when inspectors visit a declared facility and ask, for example, to see another building on the site that the IAEA does not routinely inspect. This right to quickly expanded access to declared sites was woven into the Additional Protocol in the early 1990s after revelations that work on Iraq's pre-war nuclear-weapons programme was taking place at sites the IAEA visited but at buildings inspectors did not frequent.

IAEA inspections in Iran follow the normal practice laid out in Iran's comprehensive safeguards agreement and the Additional Protocol. The provisions of the JCPOA then extend the scope of the IAEA's verification practices beyond the norm. In the words of the IAEA, the combination of its proven monitoring techniques and the requirements of the JCPOA makes for 'the most robust verification system in existence anywhere in the world'.[33]

The verification system is backed up by intelligence support from the US and other IAEA member states. Intelligence tip-offs from member states are a critical backstop in assuring the absence of undeclared secret activities – the most difficult challenge the IAEA faces in monitoring Iran's nuclear activities. If the US or other supporters of strong verification collect credible information about renewed nuclear-weapons work in Iran, they would almost certainly share it with the IAEA.

The IAEA has a track record of acting on such information. When the agency develops or receives evidence raising concerns about the nuclear activities of Iran or any other state, the required procedure is to first consult with the state in question to try to clarify anomalies. If the answers are not persuasive, the agency has the right to ask for access to undeclared sites that are not subject to regular safeguards inspections, including military sites. Prior to the JCPOA, there was no dispute-resolution process in the case where Iran balked at such a request. Under the accord, unresolved issues go for adjudication to the eight-member Joint Commission, where the US and its European allies comprised a majority. (US withdrawal from the JCPOA on 8 May 2018 reduced the Joint Commission to seven members, with European members still in the majority.) The procedures for dispute resolution are spelled out in the JCPOA, which improves upon the normal process under the IAEA Additional Protocol by setting deadlines. To date, Iran has not denied any access requests, so there have been no disputes to be resolved.

The 24-day time limit specified in the JCPOA for resolving any access dispute adds an important means of preventing the sort of delaying tactics Tehran employed before the nuclear deal. Prior to the JCPOA, there was no specified deadline at all for granting visit requests. The IAEA had been asking for three and a half years to access Parchin before Tehran allowed Amano to visit the site in September 2015. His visit and the environmental sampling at Parchin that the IAEA remotely supervised that autumn contributed to his conclusion that Iran had engaged in activities relevant to the development of a nuclear explosive device.[34]

Military sites

JCPOA critics have seized upon the aforementioned statements by senior Iranian officials ruling out inspector visits to military sites to highlight the supposed limits to verification under the deal. Amano has downplayed such statements, knowing that they are for domestic political consumption: Iranian leaders have said similar things before, then allowed visits regardless. In November 2017, Amano stressed that the agency has access to any location it needs in Iran, and that its right to access does not depend on whether a site is civilian or military.[35] There is ample precedent: before the JCPOA, the IAEA visited military sites in Iran more than 20 times.[36]

Under its confidentiality rules, the IAEA does not typically disclose details of locations visited. In 2017, the agency conducted 35 inspections in Iran under the 'complementary access' provisions of the Additional Protocol.[37] Whether any of these were military sites is not known, but that is irrelevant. What is relevant is that the IAEA states with no ambiguity that Iran has not denied any inspection access requests.

If the US or any other state has intelligence information about Iranian violations at a military site, then this information should be shared with the IAEA to help direct verification efforts. If the alleged violation could not be addressed by other means, then the IAEA would have good reason to request an inspection. On the other hand, an inspection request designed simply to trap Iran into saying no would be a subversion of the process, and the IAEA would never agree to such an unwarranted demand. Overreach by the IAEA in this regard would not only endanger the future of the JCPOA, but it would also undermine future access requests with perhaps a stronger case behind them and threaten the IAEA's credibility worldwide as it pursues incisive global verification safeguards.

After visiting IAEA headquarters in August 2017, US Ambassador to the United Nations Nikki Haley pressed the agency to seek access to Iranian military bases to ensure that no nuclear activity was being concealed.[38] Haley may have had in mind how Iraq in the 1990s sought to hide evidence of its proscribed nuclear and missile development, even when inspectors had 'anywhere, anytime' access rights. While full IAEA rights to visit military sites would be ideal for non-proliferation purposes, it is simply not realistic. No country would grant inspectors unfettered access that might threaten military security, and Russia and China strenuously object to any expansion to the inspection rights of (in their view) a Western-dominated agency. The IAEA thus reserves its site-visit requests to specific instances when it has actionable information and for which it would have the strong support of the Board of Governors.

Meanwhile, the IAEA remotely keeps watch on all locations of interest in Iran. This generic term does not mean places where there are credible indicators of undeclared nuclear activity, which would trigger an IAEA access request. It means, rather, places that could potentially be related to nuclear activity. There may be 300 such sites.[39] The IAEA does not comment on how it monitors them, but has said that it collects and analyses several million pieces of open-source information each month.[40] Much can be gleaned from scientific papers, import/export data, overhead imagery and media reporting, as well as from intelligence briefings by member states, for example. If such information points to anomalies, the IAEA then poses queries to the state. If the answers are unsatisfactory, the IAEA can request a site visit, as described above.

Section T

Much of the criticism over IAEA inspection rights revolves around the ambiguity over verification of the Section T prohibitions on four types of research activities that could contribute to the development of a nuclear explosive device. These prohibitions concern computer models to simulate nuclear explosive devices, multi-point explosive detonation systems, explosive diagnostic systems such as streak cameras, and explosively driven neutron sources. The parties could not agree on how the absence of these activities was to be verified, so it was left unstated. Iran resisted measures that would exceed the norm for other states, and it found strong support from Russia. Moscow even objected to the IAEA's statements in its quarterly reports, beginning in June 2017, that it continues to monitor and verify Section T commitments.[41] The IAEA takes the position that prohibited weaponisation development is covered by the overall verification procedures of the JCPOA.

Some critics claim that unless Iran allows inspection of military sites, Section T cannot be verified. An August 2017 report by the Washington-based Institute for Science and International Security claimed, for example, that the IAEA must ask to check the status of dual-use equipment that Iran has imported in the past.[42] Verifying the peaceful use of such equipment would reinforce confidence that at least that particular equipment is not contributing to cheating, but this is not a requirement of the JCPOA.

In September 2017, Amano, in language winced at by aides, said the IAEA's tools for verifying Section T needed 'more clarification', and that he saw no commitment from Iran to submit to IAEA monitoring for these technologies.[43] Although critics seized upon his statement as further evidence that the JCPOA is not being fully implemented,[44] Amano was mostly pushing against Russian – not Iranian – intransigence.[45]

Wary about US use of IAEA information for intelligence and military purposes, Russia has taken the legally unsupportable position that the IAEA 'has no mandate to verify Section T', in the words of Minister of Foreign Affairs Sergei Lavrov.[46] This argument flies in the face of UNSCR 2231, which asks the IAEA to verify the nuclear-related limitations of the JCPOA. The resolution does not exclude Section T from the JCPOA verification task.

PMD swept under the rug

The IAEA's inability to draw definitive conclusions on the military dimensions of Iran's past nuclear research and the compromise made to let the issue remain unresolved continues to draw flak from JCPOA critics. Iran's failure to acknowledge – much less atone for – this research suggests that it may resume nuclear-weapons development in the future. Its nuclear hedging strategy is only barely recessed. Defenders of the JCPOA respond that the deal is not based on trust in Iran's intentions, but on lack thereof: it is precisely *because* of Iran's past weaponisation work and hedging strategy that the limits and intrusive verification measures of the JCPOA are necessary.

The unsettling nature of the PMD issue was magnified on 30 April 2018 when Benjamin Netanyahu, prime minister of Israel, revealed a cache of 55,000 pages of documents and 183 CDs that Israeli intelligence had obtained from a warehouse in Tehran documenting past nuclear-weapons development work. The details went beyond what had been publicly known about that work, establishing that 'Project Ahmed' (as Iran called it) aimed to design, produce and test five ten-kilotonne warheads. The general contours were consistent with what the IAEA had already reported, but indicated that the nuclear-weapons development was more comprehensive than previously understood and went beyond exploratory work. Netanyahu presented no evidence that nuclear-weapons-related research had continued, but he accused Iran of ramping up efforts to obscure the 'atomic archive' in 2015 and moving it to the warehouse in 2017. This, he claimed, demonstrated that Iran planned to continue pursuing a nuclear-weapons programme despite the JCPOA, which he said was based on lies.[47]

In reality, the starting point for the accord was deep distrust of Iran – hence the emphasis the JCPOA placed on verification. Knowing that Iran had previously engaged in nuclear-weapons development, Western powers sought a deal with the most intrusive possible inspection arrangements to prevent Iran from advancing its nuclear hedging strategy. Former US secretary of state John Kerry, who negotiated the JCPOA, tweeted: '[e]very detail PM Netanyahu presented yesterday was every reason the world came together to apply years of sanctions and negotiate the Iran nuclear agreement – because the threat was real and had to be stopped.'[48]

After Netanyahu's presentation, the White House press secretary issued a supportive statement, saying the information was 'consistent with what the United States has long known: that Iran has a robust, clandestine nuclear weapons program that it has tried and failed to hide from the world and from its own people'.[49] The use of the present tense ('has') contradicted the assessment of the US intelligence community that Iran had suspended this programme in 2003, a fact which must have been brought to the White House's attention, as the statement was soon corrected to say that Iran 'had' a nuclear-weapons programme, with the error described as a 'typo'.[50] This discrepancy between the White House's statement and the official assessment of the United States' intelligence agencies is consistent with the views of National Security Advisor John Bolton, whom Trump appointed in March 2018. Before his appointment, Bolton had written in a private capacity about Iran's 'ongoing efforts to develop deliverable nuclear weapons'.[51] Richard Haass, president of the Council on Foreign Relations, reflected the scepticism voiced by many commentators when he wrote that the Trump administration's misstatement was 'either evidence of lack of rigorous national security process or (and much worse) the politicization of intelligence … the deliberate misrepresentation of the facts in order to justify breaking up the JCPOA'.[52] Netanyahu's slide show made a similar misstatement in using the present tense regarding Iran's nuclear-weapons programme: Israel left the mistake uncorrected for a day.

Some JCPOA critics claimed that Iran's preservation of the 'atomic archive' was a violation of the Section T prohibitions, but this accusation is a stretch. The commitments came into force only on JCPOA Implementation Day (16 January 2016) and are forward-looking: 'Iran will not engage in … [d]esigning, developing, fabricating, acquiring, or using computer models to simulate nuclear explosive devices', and so forth.[53] The documents that Israel obtained should bolster the IAEA's case for seeking access to any previously unknown nuclear-related locations that are mentioned in the archive.[54] Iran will also have to answer any new questions raised by the files if the IAEA is to be able to draw the broader conclusion.

Uranium particles at Parchin

Some analysts contend that the IAEA needs to return to Parchin to seek clarity concerning two particles picked up by environmental sampling,[55] which, according to a December 2015 IAEA report, appeared to be chemically modified natural uranium, suggesting the presence of anthropogenic uranium. The report stated that '[t]his small number of particles with such elemental composition and morphology is not sufficient to indicate a connection with the use of nuclear material'.[56]

Given the extensive refurbishment and landscaping carried out at the site since the IAEA first requested access, additional sampling would not likely shed any further clarity on the matter. In any case the IAEA, backed by intelligence information from the US and other member states, already has clear indicators of nuclear explosives work having taken place there and is in a position to verify that it is no longer taking place. The results of the 2015 sample provide a baseline against which to compare any future sampling, should the IAEA see any evidence that weapons activities have resumed at that location.

False claims of violations

In 13 reports from January 2016 through August 2018, the IAEA has verified that Iran has been keeping to the limits set by the JCPOA, with the minor exception of two small overages in heavy-water stockpiles in 2016.[57] In fact, the four reports for 2017, which included more detail than those for 2016, said the LEU stockpile was less than half the amount allowed under the deal. Despite these authoritative reports confirming Iran's adherence to the deal, critics have laboured to create a narrative of Iranian violations. Mike Pompeo, then director of the CIA, for example, reportedly told aides in spring 2017: 'we know they're cheating anyway – we're just not seeing it.'[58] The remark followed a detailed briefing to him by agency analysts, who had concluded that Iran appeared to be complying with the terms of the deal. In April and July 2017, then-secretary of state Rex Tillerson (whom Pompeo replaced in April 2018) certified in letters to Congress that Iran had met the requirements for compliance with the JCPOA. Although some critics of the JCPOA claimed that such compliance certifications did not certify compliance, White House talking points[59] and the State Department spokesperson[60] both stated that Iran was in compliance.

These judgements notwithstanding, in a speech at the conservative American Enterprise Institute in early September 2017, Haley claimed that Trump 'ha[d] grounds' to declare that Iran is not complying with the JCPOA. The only clear evidence she cited, however, was the overages of heavy water. She also claimed that Iran had refused to allow inspectors to visit military bases and mistakenly alleged that Iran has 'hundreds of undeclared sites that have suspicious activity that [inspectors] haven't looked at'.[61] This apparently was a distorted reference to the number of sites on which the IAEA keeps a watching brief.

In July 2017, Senator Cotton and three fellow Republican senators published an open letter urging Tillerson to decline to certify to Congress that Iran was complying with the JCPOA. The four senators listed 'four publicly known ways' in which Iran had violated the deal. In the letter, they said:

1) Iran is currently operating more advanced nuclear centrifuges than it is permitted under the JCPOA, maintains more advanced centrifuges than required for its permitted enrichment activities, and has announced the capability to initiate mass production of more advanced centrifuges.

2) Iran has repeatedly exceeded the limits the JCPOA places on its heavy-water stocks. Heavy water is key to Iran's plutonium pathway to nuclear weapons. However, Iran has twice exceeded the JCPOA's heavy-water cap and has claimed a right to produce unlimited amounts of heavy water and retain ownership of those stocks as long as it claims to be 'seeking' an international buyer. In doing so, Iran has effectively read the heavy-water limitation out of the JCPOA.

3) German intelligence agencies in 2015 and 2016 reported that Iran continued illicit attempts to procure nuclear and missile technology outside of JCPOA-approved channels.

4) Perhaps most concerning is Iran's refusal to grant international inspectors access to nuclear-research and military facilities. International Atomic Energy Agency ('IAEA') inspectors are entitled to visit any location in Iran to verify compliance with the JCPOA's ban on nuclear weapons development. However, Iran's refusal to grant inspectors physical access and other forms of access makes it possible – if not highly probable, given Iran's history of duplicity – that it is concealing additional violations of the JCPOA.[62]

None of these four allegations stands up to scrutiny, and it is worth examining each of them in turn. With regard to the first point, on centrifuges, there was no violation of any strict equipment limit. If there had been, the IAEA would have reported it, in accordance with its verification responsibilities. It is possible, of course, that Iran was conducting secret research, but this is not what the senators meant. The basis for their claim, rather, lay in a difference of interpretation among the JCPOA parties about how many advanced centrifuges Iran could operate for research and development purposes. The agreement specified 'roughly ten' IR-6 centrifuges. Iran claimed this could mean up to 13, while Western parties said it meant ten plus/minus one. Further discussions at the Joint Commission in 2017 settled it at 11.[63] Although Iran certainly tested the limits of the deal, it is key to note that there is no meaningful difference between ten and 13 centrifuges, in terms of contribution to Iran's knowledge about how the centrifuges perform. As for the senators' second claim, about the heavy-water overages: as noted above, the IAEA did report two instances in 2016 in which Iran briefly and by a small amount exceeded the 130 tonne limit for heavy water stockpiled. The first overage was by 0.9 metric tonnes, less than 1% of the limit; the second was 100 kg, less than 0.1% of the limit. In both cases, the extra amounts were exported to

Oman for subsequent international sale, as allowed for in the JCPOA. Paragraph 10 of the general provisions of the accord explicitly refers to limits on heavy water 'in Iran'. The overages in 2016 were unnecessary and provocative, but they did not amount to a material breach of the deal.

Commentary on these overages in the US typically neglected to explain why heavy water, which has many civilian uses, is considered sensitive. Saying only that it is 'used in the production of weapons-grade plutonium', for example, gave the impression that heavy water is a source material for nuclear weapons. Heavy water – so-called because its hydrogen atoms are weighted by an extra proton – is used, rather, to moderate the chain reaction in a certain kind of nuclear reactor. Since the JCPOA put limits on such reactors, heavy water was also limited as a supplementary precaution. With the Arak reactor disabled, Iran now possesses no such reactors. One can be reasonably certain about this because construction of new research reactors would be hard to conceal from intelligence agencies. Iran's heavy water is therefore of little current proliferation concern.

The 130-tonne limit is spelled out in paragraph 14 of Annex I of the agreement:

> All excess heavy water which is beyond Iran's needs … will be made available to export to the international market based on international prices and delivered to the international buyer for 15 years. Iran's needs, consistent with the parameters above, are estimated to be 130 metric tonnes of nuclear grade heavy water or its equivalent in different enrichments prior to commissioning of the modernised Arak research reactor, and 90 metric tonnes after the commissioning, including the amount contained in the reactor.[64]

Iran claims this limit – the 'estimated' need of 130 tonnes – is not a strict requirement because of the roundabout way in which this paragraph is written. There is no doubt, however, that Western powers considered this a firm limit during negotiations.[65] That said, no limits were agreed about the excess that could be sent elsewhere while an international purchaser is sought.

The third claim in the July 2017 letter, regarding German intelligence findings, misconstrued the facts. The illicit procurement of 'nuclear and missile technology', reported in 2015, occurred before the JCPOA was signed and the Procurement Channel established. The JCPOA does not cover the missile-related procurements reported in 2016. The senators' letter also left out a key conclusion of the relevant report by German domestic security agency the Federal Office for the Protection of the Constitution (Bundesamt für Verfassungsschutz, or BfV), which in 2016 'found significantly less evidence of Iranian attempts to acquire proliferation-sensitive material for its nuclear programme. As far as the BfV was able to verify such evidence, it did not reveal any violation of the Joint Comprehensive Plan of Action.'[66]

The fourth claim in the senators' letter – Iran's alleged 'refusal to grant international inspectors access to nuclear-research and military facilities' – is potentially the most serious, but this too was conjecture. As of the time of the letter and thereafter, Iran had not refused the agency access for JCPOA verification. It may have been the case that the IAEA had not yet sought access to military facilities because inspectors were able to answer by other means any questions that arose about Iranian activities under the JCPOA. The senators were undoubtedly referring to statements by Iranian officials that international inspectors would not be allowed on military bases. As discussed above, such statements should not be taken at face value. On several occasions Iranian officials, including the Supreme Leader, have drawn red lines from which they later backed off.

Earlier in 2017, the Institute for Science and International Security had erroneously referred to 'persistent violations' of the deal by Iran, alongside its 'exploitation of loopholes in the deal, and its pushing of the envelope of nuclear limitations'.[67] Again, the only clear breaches the Institute could point to were the two brief overages of heavy-water stockpiles. The Institute's analysis also gave a misleading impression, for example, when it said that Iran had 'exploited a loophole in the JCPOA and enriched a considerable amount of natural uranium using its existing stocks of depleted uranium'. Later, the report correctly explained that Iran had enriched depleted uranium to bring it back to the level of natural uranium (which is not the same as 'enriching natural uranium'). The analysis did not explain why this should be of significant proliferation concern, since Iran already has ample amounts of natural uranium gas and re-enrichment adds only a fraction to its stockpile.

In another report, the Institute claimed that in 2016, when the JCPOA came into effect, Iran exceeded the 300 kg limit on LEU because of the amount in sludge and other waste that the Joint Commission determined should not be counted against the limit.[68] It did not explain why hard-to-recover uranium in waste products should be a significant proliferation concern. There are far easier ways for Iran to produce LEU than through the Herculean task of recovering it from sludge. Over many years, the IAEA has never counted such waste in its determination of Iran's enriched-uranium stockpile. To suggest it should now count as part of the stockpile makes no logical or technical sense.

Iran's regional activity

Although Tehran is meeting its commitments under the JCPOA, Iran continues provocative activity in other realms. While Iran's misbehaviour is often exaggerated, its arming of Hizbullah, military intervention in Syria in support of Bashar al-Assad's regime, military support for Houthi rebels in Yemen, ballistic-missile tests, detaining of dual citizens on dubious charges and its sustained threats toward Israel are unacceptable.

As objectionable as these actions are, challenges in the nuclear field that used to loom large are no longer an issue – at least not so long as the terms of the JCPOA remain fulfilled. With Iran's nuclear programme under strict limits, the prospect of war over nuclear issues is off the table. Considering the other problems that Iran continues to pose, states beyond Iran's immediate region should prioritise their objectives. Preserving a deal that blocks all Iranian paths to a nuclear weapon is a first-order goal. Only with nuclear weapons would Iran present a direct national-security threat to states beyond its immediate neighbourhood. Impairing Iran's ballistic-missile programme is a second-order objective. Stopping Iran's arms shipments to Yemen is at best a third-order problem, the solution for which lies in an internal political settlement in Yemen and dialogue between Iran and Saudi Arabia.

Many critics of the JCPOA contend that repatriation of the unfrozen oil-sale proceeds enabled Iran to expand its activity and influence in the region at their expense: these claims are unsupported by the evidence. Iran has certainly taken advantage of opportunities presented by the failed governance of weak Arab states and the vacuum caused by Washington's desire to avoid further entanglements in the region.[69] But there is no correlation between Iran's available funds and its aggressive regional activities, as demonstrated in a comprehensive report by the International Crisis Group.[70] Testifying before Congress in April 2017, Lieutenant-General Vince Stewart, director of the US Defense Intelligence Agency, said that '[t]he preponderance of the money [had] gone to economic development and infrastructure'.[71] Rouhani had committed to addressing Iran's enormous internal needs and improving economic growth. At a May 2015 summit meeting with members of the Gulf Cooperation Council (GCC), Obama noted that most of Iran's 'destabilising activity' was low-tech and conducted at little cost, and a bigger budget would not provide a significant boost.[72]

In Pompeo's first speech as Secretary of State, delivered on 21 May 2018, what he referred to as Iran's 'rogue state actions' were a central theme. Half of the 12 demands he made of Iran pertained to its regional activities: Pompeo said that Iran must end support to 'terrorist groups', to the Houthi militia, to the Taliban and to 'militant partners around the world'; respect the sovereignty of the Iraqi government; and withdraw all its forces from Syria. He also demanded that Iran come clean about its past nuclear-weapons work, allow the IAEA unqualified access throughout the country, stop its uranium enrichment, ballistic-missile testing and transfers, and release all US citizens – and those of the United States' partners and allies – detained on spurious charges. Pompeo also called on US allies and partners around the world to join in putting 'unprecedented financial pressure' on Tehran in connection with Washington's new Iran strategy.[73]

US allies did not quibble with Pompeo regarding the desirability of Iran changing its behaviour in line with these 12 demands. Yet they doubted whether such objectives could be achieved through economic coercion and did not view them as being on a par with halting Iran's path to a nuclear weapon. Most US partners did not believe that a non-nuclear Iran threatened their vital national interests or that it was uniquely at fault in the region. Here, Pompeo aligned US priorities with those of Israel and Saudi Arabia, and set his country at odds with partners on which Washington had relied to enforce sanctions and craft the JCPOA.

US withdrawal

False accusations of Iranian violations served to validate Trump's claims before and after his election that the JCPOA was the 'worst deal ever'. It took 16 months, however, before he took decisive action to withdraw from the agreement. The president of the United States has the authority at any time to issue an executive order applying new sanctions or reapplying old ones that were eased under the JCPOA. Trump could not unilaterally carry out his election pledge to 'rip up' the multilateral agreement if the other seven parties wanted to preserve it, but he could end the waivers of US sanctions that provided the largest trade-off for the compromises Iran was making.

Trump also faced a set timetable under US law to determine every few months whether to continue to waive nuclear-related sanctions as called for by the JCPOA. Some of the waivers had a four-month timetable, others six months. During his first year in office, Trump reluctantly issued the waivers, encouraged to do so by Tillerson, then-national security advisor H.R. McMaster and Secretary of Defense James Mattis. While all three were highly critical of Iran, they saw value in maintaining the JCPOA as long as Iran was abiding by its provisions.

Separate from the timetable for sanctions waivers, the president was also required by the Iran Nuclear Agreement Review Act of 2015 to certify every 90 days that Iran was implementing the agreement and that suspension of sanctions was vital to US national-security interests. This certification requirement was set in 2015 as a condition for congressional acquiescence to the JCPOA.[74]

The separate deadlines for continuing to waive sanctions under the JCPOA and certification under US law of Iranian compliance contributed to confusing decisions. In September 2017, Trump waived the sanctions once again. The next month, however, he decided not to issue the certification. Rather than claiming Iranian non-compliance, Trump said instead that he could not certify that the suspension of sanctions under the deal was 'appropriate and proportionate', as specified by the aforementioned Act. Framing this as a chance to work with Congress to redress perceived flaws in the deal, Trump warned 'in the event we are not able to reach a solution working with Congress and our allies, then the agreement will be terminated'.[75] In January 2018, however, he again waived sanctions, giving Congress one last chance. It was easier to end certification than the sanctions waiver, because the former had no legal bearing on the JCPOA. Ending the sanctions waivers, on the other hand, would be a material breach of the agreement.

In mid-January 2018, the deadlines for decisions on certification and sanctions waivers coincided. As in the autumn, Trump again suspended sanctions but did not certify Iranian compliance. In doing so, he insisted that it would be the last time he waived sanctions unless Congress passed new legislation that would, among other provisions, require Iran to allow 'immediate inspections at all sites requested by international inspectors', ensure Iran never comes close to possessing nuclear weapons, remove the expiration dates from the limits that the JCPOA set on Iran's nuclear programme and subject any missile testing by Iran to 'severe sanctions'. He also called on European partners to 'fix' the deal by addressing these perceived shortcomings (the second and third of which were essentially the same), and to take steps 'to confront Iran's other malign activities'.[76]

As the next deadline for sanctions waivers approached (12 May), European partners made an all-out effort to persuade Trump to honour the United States' commitments under the deal. French President Emmanuel Macron came to Washington to try to leverage the bonhomie he had established with his US counterpart. German Chancellor Angela Merkel also came, with less pomp but equal belief in the security, peace and non-proliferation benefits of the JCPOA. Boris Johnson, then UK foreign secretary, also visited Washington, and UK Prime Minister Theresa May made similar arguments in telephone calls with Trump.

Meanwhile, diplomats from Western parties to the JCPOA had been working intently with their counterparts in the State Department to address Trump's demands. They came very close to consensus on a package that would complement the JCPOA. The allies would confirm the right of the IAEA to conduct inspections anywhere it has reason to believe nuclear activity might be taking place, and they would declare that any Iranian long-range missile development would trigger strong pushback. Trump's demand to abolish the JCPOA's sunset provisions on nuclear enrichment were the most difficult issue, because imposing permanent restrictions on Iran's enrichment capacity was an obvious deal breaker for Iran. France, Germany and the United Kingdom knew that Iran would not accept unprecedented and perpetual limits. The diplomats came up with a way, however, to have the limits extended on a voluntary basis. They would declare that if Iran's future nuclear capabilities were not proportional to its civilian energy programme, they would reserve the right to reimpose sanctions. Given that Russia had agreed to supply fuel for the reactors it provides, Iran would not need an industrial-sized enrichment programme for the foreseeable future, they judged. A fourth pillar of the supplemental agreement among the allies would address Iran's regional military activity in Syria and Yemen by sanctioning Iranian militias and commanders intervening in either country or involved in missile transfers.[77]

Efforts to meet Trump halfway were fruitless. Calling it 'insane' to oppose agreements recently entered into, Macron said at the end of his trip that Trump was set to pull out of the deal as part of 'a strategy of increasing tension' and for domestic political reasons.[78] Trump's hawkish new security team reinforced his political inclinations. On 9 April, former ambassador to the UN John Bolton took over as National Security Advisor, replacing McMaster. Bolton had been a long-time advocate for regime change in Iran, which he has called the 'only long-term solution' to the threats posed by the country,[79] and for the termination of the JCPOA, rather than trying to improve it.[80] Long before Trump's election, in the final months of negotiations on the JCPOA, Bolton advocated military action as the only way to stop Iran's nuclear programme.[81] Pompeo, too, had previously argued for regime change in Iran: as a member of the House of Representatives, Pompeo had called upon Congress to 'change Iranian behavior, and ultimately, the Iranian regime'.[82]

Administration officials found it hard to explain Trump's decision. In background briefings to explain the strategy, State Department officials had no good answers about the purpose of reimposing sanctions on Iran, what it was expected to achieve and what would replace the JCPOA.[83] At a briefing delivered the day Trump announced the US withdrawal, a State Department official attempting to explain why pulling out entirely was better than the package nearly negotiated with the E3 could say only that:

> it's a cost–benefit analysis, right? I mean, if you get X value from the – where we got to with the Europeans and then you add the kind of negative value that Iran gets from using the protections alluded – endogenous to the deal to project power in the region, it comes out to less than the benefit you get from getting out. I think that's – that's the way we look at it.

Pressed further, it did not seem that the State Department had a clear idea of how Europe would react.[84]

Trump's withdrawal immediately isolated the US. Apart from four states in the Middle East – Bahrain, Israel, Saudi Arabia and the United Arab Emirates – the reaction was alarm and despair. Europeans, in particular, were dismayed over the assault on one of the EU's greatest foreign-policy achievements and the secondary sanctions that Trump threatened to impose on their firms doing lawful business with Iran. Pouring salt in the wound, US Ambassador to Germany Richard Grenell in his first day on the job on 8 May doubled down on US demands, tweeting that 'German companies doing business in Iran should wind down operations immediately'.[85] European Council President Donald Tusk summed up the mood when he condemned the 'capricious assertiveness of the American administration', and tweeted: 'with friends like that who needs enemies'.[86] The transatlantic rift looked to be at its widest in decades.

Regime-change strategy?

The 'strategy' that Pompeo rolled out did not speak of war, except in an economic and financial sense. It is not a viable strategy, however, in that it was based on the assumption that US allies and partners would rally behind the US, despite their expressed opposition to such a course of action. Even before Trump's withdrawal from the JCPOA, Washington was successful in bullying foreign firms into forgoing trade with Iran so as not to risk access to US markets. One survey of senior managers at multinational companies conducted in 2017 indicated that 79% of companies had delayed their plans for doing business in Iran since the deal's implementation: 57% identified the fear of US sanctions reimposition as their primary reason for doing so.[87] But very few states voluntarily joined in reapplying sanctions that were lifted in exchange for Iran's well-documented adherence to the nuclear deal.

Some states also worried that Trump's hidden objective was not the stated goal of behaviour change, but rather regime change. Pompeo hinted at this in a press conference after his speech on 21 May when he said:

> At the end of the day, the Iranian people will get to make a choice about their leadership. If they make the decision quickly, that would be wonderful. If they choose not to do so, we will stay hard at this until we achieve the outcomes that I set forward today.[88]

Popular protests that engulfed many Iranian cities beginning in December 2017 fanned hopes in some quarters in Washington that regime change was on its way and that killing the JCPOA would accelerate this process.[89] This was a misreading of the domestic mood in Iran. While some protesters did voice anger at not seeing the promised benefits of the deal, they were not denouncing the JCPOA at large, and they were certainly not calling for foreign sanctions against Iran. Contradicting claims by the Trump administration that the protesters would be encouraged by vocal US support,[90] an opinion poll in Iran conducted in mid-January found that 87% agreed that Trump's expressions of support for the protesters had either hurt the protesters (39%) or had no effect (48%).[91] Notwithstanding doubts about the trustworthiness of opinion polling in Iran, there is no counter evidence to suggest that these results are false.

While some protesters chanted 'death to the dictator' (a reference to Khamenei), most did not appear to be seeking a fundamental change to the system. Reports from Iran tell a mixed story about what motivated the protests. While they undermined claims of regime cohesion, it is too early to conclude that a majority of Iranians are dissatisfied with the government's regional policies or its domestic priorities. Polling from summer 2017 in fact suggests otherwise.[92]

The JCPOA after US withdrawal

Whether ending the waivers will kill the deal is unclear; it depends on the remaining parties. The EU has taken a number of steps to protect both the deal and European firms from the impact of US sanctions. One step was to update its Blocking Statute – introduced in 1996 to protect European companies from US sanctions on Cuba, Iran and Libya, though never enacted – that prohibits EU individuals and organisations complying with US secondary sanctions and allows for the recovery in EU courts of any damages suffered as a result. While the Blocking Statute, which entered into force in August 2018, does not offer complete protection, in that implementation depends on action by the individual EU members, Brussels could supplement it by launching a dispute-settlement procedure against the US at the World Trade Organization.[93] In early September 2018, EU High Representative Federica Mogherini announced that the EU would establish a new mechanism, a 'Special Purpose Vehicle', to facilitate legitimate trade with Iran outside US financial reach.[94] In a joint statement on 2 November, Mogherini and the E3 foreign and finance ministers committed themselves to 'enable continued sanctions lifting to reach Iran'.[95]

Tehran will have to decide whether the benefits from trade that escapes US secondary sanctions justify intrusive inspections and limits on fissile-material production. Tehran would also need to factor in the possibility of a US, Israeli or joint military strike if it were to rapidly ramp up its enrichment capability to the level seen before the agreement of the JCPOA. A push by Iranian hardliners to pull out of the NPT[96] – thereby dropping any pretence about its purely peaceful use of nuclear energy –

would have to be weighed against the risk that it would prompt a military reaction. Rather than moves that would immediately shorten the breakout period, Iran's more likely response, if it decided to reduce adherence to the JCPOA, would be to restrict IAEA inspections and ramp up research and development of more efficient centrifuges. Doing so might encourage Saudi Arabia to seek a nuclear hedging strategy of its own. Iran could also take retaliatory moves in non-nuclear areas, such as detaining more US citizens and being more aggressive towards Israel. Trump's move could therefore heighten regional tensions and increase the likelihood of a nuclear-arms race.

Conclusions

The JCPOA was far from perfect, and the unsettled issue of Iran's past nuclear-weapons development left an indelible blemish. It involved compromises, like any negotiated agreement. Before the US withdrawal, however, it was running smoothly. Iran was honouring its commitments and minor issues were being resolved. If left in place, JCPOA implementation could be further improved in ways that do not require renegotiation of the deal itself. The Joint Commission established under the JCPOA to address complaints and ambiguities has had success in deciding on technical issues that were left undefined, such as the number of advanced centrifuges Iran is allowed to operate for research and development purposes. The Joint Commission should continue to ensure that the IAEA can conduct uninterrupted monitoring of this work. The Joint Commission should also clarify the role of the IAEA in verifying the unprecedented restrictions that the JCPOA imposed on certain activities that would contribute to nuclear-weapons development. Iran's production of more heavy water than needed for domestic purposes should also be addressed. Exporting the excess to Oman for storage is an unnecessary encouragement to Iran's nuclear-export dreams; the commercial market for the heavy water is limited anyway. It would be good to tighten the limits on heavy water, so that they apply to excess product sent elsewhere for storage prior to sale. However, these issues, which Haley and Republican senators have blown way out of proportion, are minor, compared to the peril now facing the JCPOA.

Iran's military facilities should not be off-limits for the IAEA; as noted above, inspectors have visited Iranian military sites more than 20 times. They have apparently not done so, however, in the first two to three years of the JCPOA. It is important that this should not become the norm. In any case, military-site visits will be required for the IAEA to affirm the broader conclusion. To do so, the IAEA would need to put firmly to rest all lingering concerns about Parchin and any other military sites where past nuclear activity is suspected. Iran has good reason to cooperate with the IAEA in allowing military-site visits: it wants the legitimacy that the broader conclusion would confer.

Countries concerned about Iran should remain vigilant. Thanks to the balanced deal struck with Iran in July 2015, Iran's nuclear programme has been limited and tightly inspected. The IAEA's vigilant verification of the JCPOA remains the best way to ensure that Iran does not engage in military nuclear activity. While JCPOA limits on enrichment will expire in about a decade, the enhanced verification measures are permanent. As Amano said in November 2017, 'the sun does not set on IAEA safeguards'.[97]

It should be clear that more sanctions will not cause Iran to buckle under and renegotiate the JCPOA on US terms, especially when no other major partner voluntarily supports new penalties. Sanctions helped bring Iran to the negotiating table, but they are not what persuaded it to cut back its nuclear infrastructure and accept intrusive inspections. Rather,

US willingness to compromise by accepting some level of enrichment in Iran was key to persuading Iran to accept limits. Without the compromise, there would have been no deal.

The case of North Korea shows how abandoning a deal that limited its plutonium production has led to an insurmountable problem. The 1994 Agreed Framework was not perfect and North Korea cheated, but the deal did significantly roll back its nuclear-weapons programme. Similarly, in Iran's case, it is far better to implement an incomplete but effective agreement than it is to scrap it in hopes of achieving the best outcome and end up with the worst.

CHAPTER TWO

The JCPOA Procurement Channel[1]

Paulina Izewicz

Introduction

One benefit of the Joint Comprehensive Plan of Action (JCPOA) that would be lost if the agreement fails is the oversight it provides on Iran's nuclear-related procurement. Iran's nuclear black-market trafficking, which began in the mid-1980s, gave it a head start in uranium enrichment and sources for goods and technologies to advance its nuclear aspirations. The JCPOA, agreed on 14 July 2015, sought to curb the challenge posed to both regional security and the global non-proliferation regime by establishing a dedicated mechanism through which Iran could legally procure goods for its now limited programme. Officially known as the Procurement Channel, its purpose is to review proposals by states seeking to engage in trade with Iran in goods and services involving nuclear and non-nuclear civilian end uses. This mechanism has been in place since JCPOA Implementation Day (16 January 2016), and, if the JCPOA remains in place, will remain so until Termination Day in October 2025. The withdrawal of the United States from the deal now endangers this significant achievement.

This chapter examines the mechanism in depth, seeking to answer whether it is capable, in conjunction with other tools, of curbing Iran's covert procurement of nuclear and dual-use goods. For the channel to work as intended, three basic requirements need to be met. Firstly, the Procurement Channel needs to function in practice, allowing Iran to purchase the items it justifiably needs. Secondly, it needs to be accompanied by a credible enforcement mechanism which will deter covert procurement. And thirdly, to continue adhering to restrictions on procurement, Iran needs to believe that the broader nuclear deal, of which the Procurement Channel forms part, continues to serve its interests.

This chapter explores each of these three areas in turn, devoting considerable attention to the factors behind the relatively low level of activity in the Procurement Channel to date. In doing so, what follows draws primarily on interviews with industry representatives, and current and former government officials. Beyond that, because of the strict confidentiality rules applied to the Procurement Channel process, this chapter necessarily relies on information available in the public domain.

Background

Iran has a long history of procuring nuclear-relevant technologies from abroad. It is often forgotten that some of these were legitimate purchases for civilian purposes. In 1957, under the 'Atoms for Peace' programme, for instance, the US supplied Iran with a five-megawatt nuclear research reactor – now known as the Tehran Research Reactor – along with the necessary fuel. In 1975, the Atomic Energy Organization of Iran (AEOI) concluded an agreement with the Massachusetts Institute of Technology, which trained Iran's first nuclear engineers.[2] China and Russia both played a part in building key elements of Iran's nuclear infrastructure: in the 1990s, China supplied uranium-processing capabilities, and, later in the same decade, Russian assistance helped Iran begin construction of the heavy-water production plant at Arak. Russia also took over construction of the Bushehr nuclear plant, which Germany had begun in the 1970s under the Shah. However, assistance from the US and other Western states abruptly ceased after the Iranian Revolution in 1979. Apart from Russian support for Bushehr, most other foreign assistance also dried up over time, due to pressure from the US.

In 1985, the AEOI initiated a centrifuge uranium-enrichment programme, and turned to the notorious black-market network of A.Q. Khan to purchase designs and components for P-1 and P-2 centrifuges in the late 1980s and mid-1990s.[3] This was a covert effort which only came to public attention in 2002, when Iranian exile group the National Council of Resistance of Iran revealed the existence of two undeclared nuclear sites in Iran: a uranium-enrichment plant at Natanz, and a heavy-water plant at Arak. These revelations precipitated a prolonged diplomatic crisis during which Iran continued to covertly procure goods for its nuclear programme, despite the adoption of successive United Nations Security Council resolutions from 2006–10 aimed at curbing these efforts.[4]

Iran has also sought to develop a range of technical capabilities indigenously, with mixed results. In some key areas, Iran appears to remain reliant on foreign procurement. The UN Panel of Experts – the body tasked until January 2016 with monitoring the implementation of UN sanctions on Iran – judged that Iran's procurement priorities included carbon fibre, high-strength aluminium alloys, maraging steel (an alloy with superior strength and toughness that remains malleable) and high-quality valves – materials vital to centrifuge production.[5] In some cases, it appears that Iran is unable to manufacture the necessary items to a sufficient standard for use in its nuclear programme. In other cases, Iran can probably make the items in question but engages in what outside experts have called a form of 'brand snobbery', manifested in a preference for Western-made goods.[6] In a 2014 review of known cases of illicit procurement by Iran, for instance, the King's College London-based Project Alpha found that in 147 cases where the country of origin was known, 70 of the targeted companies were European – 24 of these were German, and 21 cases involved manufacturers from the United Kingdom – and 36 cases involved US manufacturers despite the risks and difficulties inherent in such attempts.[7]

The Procurement Channel was set up as a legitimate alternative to the black market and as a way to monitor Iran's nuclear-related procurement. The channel's mandate is to review proposals from states seeking to engage in trade with Iran involving goods and services for nuclear and non-nuclear civilian end uses. Prior to the JCPOA, UN Security Council resolutions had prohibited such trade. The JCPOA changed this, allowing transfers of nuclear or dual-use goods, technology and related services, provided that the Security Council gives its approval, on a case-by-case basis.

The Procurement Channel

Scope
The Procurement Channel covers three categories of goods, and associated assistance and services.[8] The first category covers goods that are 'especially designed or prepared for nuclear use'. Most obviously, such items include complete systems such as nuclear reactors, reprocessing plants and complete centrifuges, but this category also encompasses a wide variety of parts and components. These items are listed in the Nuclear Suppliers Group's (NSG) so-called 'trigger list' (INFCIRC/254/Part 1).[9]

The second category includes goods with both nuclear and civilian applications, listed in the NSG's dual-use list (INFCIRC/254/Part 2). This category of goods is generally more difficult to control, because it includes items which, in addition to their more sensitive use, also have wide industrial and commercial applications. Goods on this list have comprised the bulk of Iran's procurement.

The third category comprises 'further items' that any state determines 'could contribute to reprocessing or enrichment-related or heavy-water-related activities inconsistent with the JCPOA'. This is akin to catch-all provisions in many national export-control regimes, which anticipate less straightforward cases. These items typically have lower technical specifications than would normally be used in a nuclear programme. They do, however, have the obvious advantage of being easier to procure, and often can be modified after purchase to make them useable in a nuclear programme. Indeed, Iran's procurers have often focused on such goods since export-control enforcement has made purchasing other goods much more difficult.[10]

The Procurement Channel also covers associated assistance and services, which include technical assistance or training, financial assistance, investment and brokering. The acquisition by Iran of an interest in commercial nuclear-related activity in foreign countries, which was previously prohibited, is also subject to the Procurement Channel.

States do not need to seek the approval of the Security Council for the supply, sale or transfer to Iran of goods and services for the JCPOA-mandated modifications of Iran's nuclear facilities at Arak and Fordow. Nor do states need to go through the Procurement Channel for the exchange for natural uranium of Iran's low-enriched uranium (LEU) in excess of the 300-kilogram JCPOA limit. Secondly, this exemption covers the provision of single- and dual-use goods for use in light-water reactors, including LEU fuel elements. This exemption is particularly salient for Russia, which is involved in the expansion of the plant at Bushehr. However, states involved in supplying items for these exempted purposes still need to notify the Security Council and Joint Commission in advance and to verify end use.

Procedure

To export any of the covered items to Iran, companies must go through the established licensing process in their home country while also submitting documents required by the Procurement Channel. The national licensing body conducts an initial review and, if the application meets the licensing criteria, forwards it to the Procurement Channel. In practice, this is done through the country's UN mission, with materials sent to a dedicated email address. The Security Council then forwards the application to the Procurement Working Group (PWG), the composition of which mirrors that of the Joint Commission (the body overseeing the implementation of the JCPOA), and, if the items are intended for a nuclear application, also to the International Atomic Energy Agency (IAEA). The PWG meets every three weeks to review proposals; the IAEA can also attend as an observer if the applications under review cover nuclear goods. If the application requires translation – proposals can be submitted in any of the UN's six official languages – this will be done by the UN Secretariat before the review process begins.

Each PWG member has 20 working days to review the proposal; if more time is required, this can be extended by ten days. Some experts have raised concerns about this timeline, which they consider too short to conduct a proper review. This time concern is perhaps most pressing in the United States, where a typical review process involves several government agencies, which necessarily requires more time. In other countries this process is generally more streamlined.[11] In light of the US withdrawal, this concern has become less relevant.

At the end of this period, if no member dissents, the PWG will recommend to the Security Council that the application be approved. If there is no consensus, Iran, with the support of one other member, can refer the case to the Joint Commission within five days; the Commission will then have ten days to consider it. The Security Council, in turn, has five working days to make a final decision. All in all, the process can take up to 50 working days. Only then, in line with the Security Council decision, can the national licensing body grant the final licence.

Proposals must contain certain specific information, largely in line with standard export-control practice. This includes technical specifications; information identifying parties (exporter, importer, end user, as well as all other entities involved in the transaction, such as agents, brokers, first consignees or freight forwarders); end use; and end-use location. An optional application form is available to help with these requirements. Incomplete proposals are likely to be disapproved, but amended applications can be resubmitted. The proposal should be accompanied by any additional documentation which would be helpful in assessing the application, such as a product catalogue, data sheets, diagrams or pictures.

Helpfully, a single proposal can cover multiple line items – that is, the supply of several goods, or the supply of goods together with related services, such as financing, transportation or insurance. The Procurement Channel guidelines acknowledge that information about such services is not always available at the time of submission, but it does need to be provided before the activity takes places as a condition for approval. Several countries can also be involved in one transaction without the need to submit separate applications, provided that they are all listed in the proposal.

All this follows a fairly routine approach, similar to typical export control regimes – with one exception. The Procurement Channel takes a rigorous approach to end-use verification. Whereas end-use certifications involving other countries are normally issued by the importing entity, the Iranian government now assumes ultimate responsibility for goods imported through the Procurement Channel. For goods intended for Iran's nuclear programme, this certification is issued by the AEOI, while the Ministry of Industry, Mine and Trade provides certificates for dual-use items. This requirement is different from typical export control regimes in that it makes the Iranian government ultimately responsible for ensuring that no goods purchased through the Procurement Channel are diverted to illicit use. Moreover, the exporting state assumes responsibility for conducting end-use verification, and the Iranian government explicitly commits to allow this verification. In the application, the proposing state is asked to confirm that it is in a position to effectively verify end use and end-use location, and it can, as a supplement, provide additional information on how it intends to conduct this verification, including measures agreed with Iran and the importing entity.[12] If the proposing state is not in a position to do so, it can request assistance from the Joint Commission; the Commission can also provide such oversight if it deems it necessary as a condition for approval. If the items are intended for nuclear use, the IAEA is charged with verifying their stated end use. Once the items are transferred, the exporting state has to notify the Security Council within ten days and also, for goods with a nuclear application, the IAEA.

Implementation to date

When the implementation of the Procurement Channel was set to begin, there was widespread concern that the mechanism would not be able to cope with the number of proposals submitted. In practice, however, this number has been significantly lower than expected. In the first six months of the Channel's functioning, from January to July 2016, only one proposal, for a temporary export of a dual-use item, was submitted (it was subsequently withdrawn). In the next six-month period, however, activity picked up. As of June 2018, 37 proposals had been submitted, 24 of which were approved, three denied, seven withdrawn and three still under review. Interestingly, 13 new proposals were submitted in the six-month period ending in June 2018, when the JCPOA was increasingly coming under threat from the Trump administration.[13] This ongoing, and indeed increased, use of the channel underscores the attachment that states have to the accord and to the legitimate process for nuclear-related trade with Iran.

Procurement Channel procedures are governed by strict confidentiality, and there is therefore little information available in the public domain about denied and withdrawn applications. Proposals would likely be rejected if there were concerns over the stockpiling of sensitive goods, or if it they were deemed inconsistent with the JCPOA; as mentioned, an incomplete application would also likely be denied. Among the known cases is a submission by an Austrian company for a temporary exhibit of a machine tool, which was later withdrawn because the company was not aware that it had to obtain an end-user certificate.[14] On another occasion, an application is understood to have been successfully discouraged before it was even submitted: in spring 2017, Iran sought to sign an agreement with Kazakhstan for the purchase of 950 tonnes of Kazakhstan's yellowcake uranium over three years; the plan was met with opposition from the United Kingdom, which ultimately prevented the deal from going through.[15]

As of December 2017, proposals had come from four different states, representing three UN regional groupings: the

Asia-Pacific (three), Eastern Europe (three) and Western Europe and Others (18).[16] In the most recent reporting period, one additional European country is understood to have begun utilising the Procurement Channel. Items sought included machine tools, measurement devices, electrical equipment, materials and pumps. The recipient industries included automotive; construction; pharmaceutical; medical; packaging; oil, gas and petrochemical; healthcare; and civil-nuclear programmes.[17] These proposals were processed, on average, in less than 51 calendar days.[18]

Can the Procurement Channel stop Iran's illicit procurement?

Obstacles to implementation
Although activity in the Procurement Channel has picked up over time, it is still lower than many policymakers and commentators had anticipated. There are several overlapping reasons for this. The initial slow rate of submissions to the Procurement Channel can largely be attributed to administrative delays on the part of Iran. The mechanism was one of the last elements of the JCPOA to be agreed, and other issues took priority ahead of Implementation Day. As a result, it took Iran a while to establish the internal mechanisms necessary for issuing end-user certificates. It was not initially clear which governmental body or bodies would be responsible for issuing these; it reportedly took four months for Iran to designate the Ministry of Industry, Mine and Trade as the entity responsible for JCPOA-controlled items.[19]

Other states also had to adjust their internal procedures, and then communicate these to their business communities. Not all of them have done so equally effectively, however, and lack of awareness of the Procurement Channel is one of the hurdles that persists. Some states, such as the UK, have made the necessary information easily available to potential sellers, and at times in more detail than that provided by the official Procurement Channel guidelines.[20] Most countries, however, have taken only limited steps to make this information available. In some cases, only abbreviated information in national languages is available, and it is often difficult to find. In other cases, national export control authorities have limited themselves to uploading English-language guidance on their websites, with no additional information provided. In yet other cases, national authorities themselves appear unaware of the Procurement Channel and its requirements.

In Iran, too, confusion is inevitable given the new requirements and the imprecise rules that typically govern business–government interactions there. In any country, it is not typically incumbent upon companies to know the control status of the goods they seek to purchase. The Procurement Channel imposes this requirement on Iranian companies, tasking them with obtaining end-use certificates. Iran has never had an export-control regime, and its bureaucracy is notoriously byzantine – lack of awareness was bound to be an issue.

Indeed, the UN secretary-general's December 2017 report on the implementation of Resolution 2231 identified lack of awareness as a major issue hindering trade through the Procurement Channel. Prior to the JCPOA, the UN Panel of Experts on Iran was the body tasked with conducting outreach to governments and the private sector. During the negotiations, Iran, keen on shedding all sanctions trappings, requested that the Panel be dissolved. It was disbanded on Implementation Day, and in its place, the UN Secretariat took on a broadly similar mandate, which also includes supporting the Procurement Channel. In that capacity, the Secretariat maintains a website where detailed information about the mechanism is available.[21] Judging by the statistics provided by a report of the facilitator on UN Security

Council Resolution (UNSCR) 2231 published in June 2018, it appears that the website is visited with reasonable, and seemingly growing, frequency: the report cited 194,000 visits as of June 2017, 250,000 as of December 2017 and 67,000 visits in the following six months.[22] But in-person outreach is critical, and because of institutional, budgetary and personnel constraints, the Secretariat is not so well positioned to undertake this effort. Indeed, since the dissolution of the Panel of Experts, the Secretariat was only able to conduct formal outreach on a handful of occasions over the past two and a half years, for the most part relying on the support of non-governmental experts. In that sense, Iran may have done itself a disservice when it insisted upon the dissolution of the Panel.

The other main reason for the low number of applications identified in the secretary-general's December 2017 report was uncertainty over the JCPOA's future. Donald Trump's election as US president put the agreement on shaky ground. His antipathy to the deal grew over the course of 2017, reaching the point where in May 2018 he stopped waiving sanctions and withdrew from the agreement. Entities worldwide that do business with Iran have since faced the prospect of US extraterritorial sanctions.

Even before Trump's decision to end US involvement in the JCPOA, sanctions exposure remained an important consideration for entities potentially interested in trade with Iran. Although the bulk of measures formerly issued by the United Nations and the European Union eased under the JCPOA, most US sanctions remained in place. As a result, US companies have been broadly prohibited from doing business with Iran, with some limited exceptions. Foreign subsidiaries of US firms, if they were sufficiently walled off from US connections, were allowed to trade with Iran. In practice, however, the costs of creating such a segregated system that met the attendant compliance procedures often acted as a deterrent to trade. Moreover, many items are designed and manufactured in the United States, or manufactured abroad based on US technology, which means they remain subject to US law. For many companies, navigating such a complex compliance landscape was already too risky and expensive, and often outweighed potential benefits. Financing transactions also remained a major issue, with many banks wary of conducting business involving Iran.

Some of these companies have also been burned by Iran's past attempts to illicitly procure sensitive goods. They were either the target of such attempts themselves, or witnessed it happen to others. As a result, they have made a conscious decision to forgo Iran as a potential market. Some reportedly receive inquiries on behalf of Iranian customers fairly frequently, but choose not to respond.

Companies have also become increasingly concerned with reputational risk. In an atmosphere of uncertainty, where legal requirements can change at any time, such concerns naturally rise in prominence. These concerns include issues as broad as human rights, as well as more specific nuclear-related considerations. On several occasions, parsing photographs of nuclear facilities and equipment released by the Iranian government, Western analysts have been able to identify a wide range of foreign-made items, including by brand.[23] This is hardly the type of advertising Western manufacturers desire, particularly if Iran's nuclear programme were to be placed once again under international sanctions in the event of JCPOA breakdown.

Geopolitical considerations also play a role in how national governments approach nuclear and dual-use exports. Iran's nuclear programme remains a politically sensitive issue, and countries may at times be hesitant to put forward proposals for consideration in the Procurement Channel. In one example in September 2017, the lower house of the Czech parliament refused to lift a ban on exports to the Bushehr nuclear power plant. While this has subsequently been overturned, members of parliament who voted against nullifying the law argued that it could harm relations with Israel.[24] Although, strictly speaking, this particular type of export would not be subject to the Procurement Channel because of its exception for light-water reactors, it is likely an example of some of the considerations with which governments must contend.

The requirement to conduct end-use verification also appears to be intimidating to some states. Very few countries routinely perform such checks as part of their national export-control regimes, typically utilising dedicated personnel or embassy staff. For many countries, however, such a task would be a novel undertaking and require resources they simply do not have. The Procurement Channel offers assistance in such instances, through the provision of experts and expertise, but the requirements themselves, as well as the process for seeking assistance, needs further demystification.

Another plausible explanation for the low application numbers is that demand in Iran has fallen short of expectations. This seems largely true of the nuclear programme, which the JCPOA has significantly constrained. It now requires fewer goods and, in some key areas such as centrifuge enrichment, is able to fall back on spare parts placed in storage. In other areas, items destined for light-water reactors or the modifications at Fordow and Arak are exempt from the Procurement Channel process. Iran has also made significant strides towards self-reliance in many industries, indigenising production or altering production lines to eliminate items which proved too difficult to obtain. A return to international procurement may take some time, and would require not only a change in mindset but also the (re-)establishment of relations with business partners.

It is also possible that Iranian companies are equally concerned about sanctions snap-back, which would curtail their access to warranty and spare parts after initial purchase.

Illicit Iranian procurement

According to a 2014 report by the UN Panel of Experts, Iran's illicit procurement appeared to have slowed down from mid-2013, when negotiations over its nuclear programme began.[25] In 2015, the Panel noted that it had not received any information about Iran's covert procurement, but added the caveat that this 'could reflect a general reduction of procurement activities by the Iranian side or a political decision by some Member States to refrain from reporting to avoid any possible negative impact on ongoing negotiations'. As the report notes, some member states continued to observe Iranian activity, assessing that it remained 'basically unchanged' and that Iran continued to procure below-threshold items.[26]

In 2016, German domestic security agency the Federal Office for the Protection of the Constitution (Bundesamt für Verfassungsschutz, or BfV) issued a report which stated that Iran's 'illegal proliferation-sensitive procurement activities in Germany … persisted in 2015 at what is, even by international standards, a quantitatively high level. This holds true in particular with regard to items which can be used in the field of nuclear technology.' The BfV also noted 'a further increase in the already considerable procurement efforts in connection with Iran's ambitious missile technology programme which could among other things potentially serve to deliver nuclear weapons'.[27]

However, the report covering the year 2016, when JCPOA implementation started, concluded:

> In 2016, the BfV found significantly less evidence of Iranian attempts to acquire proliferation-sensitive

material for its nuclear programme. As far as the BfV was able to verify such evidence, it did not reveal any violation of the Joint Comprehensive Plan of Action. The amount of evidence found for attempts to acquire proliferation-sensitive material for missile technology/the missile programme, which is not covered by the Joint Comprehensive Plan of Action, remained about the same.[28]

Several reports by German state intelligence agencies were issued around the same time, seemingly at odds with this conclusion.[29] Upon closer examination, however, these reports do not make any specific allegations with respect to Iran's nuclear programme, focusing rather on its ballistic-missile programme, or treating Iran in aggregate with countries such as North Korea. One nuclear-specific mention refers to the purchase of valves for the Arak reactor; it is, however, in the context of charges being filed in a case which predated the JCPOA by some years. These reports sparked some controversy, ultimately leading the UN Secretariat, in November 2017, to seek clarification from the German government. In response, Berlin stated that it had no indication of any activities inconsistent with Iran's nuclear-related commitments.[30]

All reports on the implementation of Resolution 2231 issued by the secretary-general from 2016 through 2017 stated that the Secretariat had not received any reports that would indicate Iranian attempts to procure nuclear and dual-use items covertly. This was, of course, not a definitive assessment that such procurement has not taken place. In response to increasingly biting sanctions over the years, Iran's procurement efforts became increasingly sophisticated, employing a wide array of concealment methods, making use of front companies and intermediaries, false documentation and new geographical

between control regimes. Certain goods covered by the Procurement Channel have multiple applications. Carbon fibre is one such item: it is controlled by both the NSG and the Missile Technology Control Regime (MTCR). According to the Procurement Channel guidelines, if an item falls under both frameworks, an application for its transfer to Iran should be submitted in accordance with the Procurement Channel procedures. The technical specifications of the material differ slightly under each regime, but these differences are not always obvious without laboratory testing. In several cases investigated by the Panel of Experts, the intended end use could be determined based on the documentation included in the shipment, but this proved impossible in some cases. In principle, it may be possible to determine end use based on the recipient, if known. In the case of the carbon-fibre shipment, the US identified the recipient as an Iranian firm that 'supports the ballistic missile programme', and considered the transfer a violation of UNSCR 2231 provisions on missile-related trans-fers.[32] Iran's ballistic-missile programme falls outside the scope of the JCPOA, and there is little reason to believe the country's procurement in this area will cease, given Iran's antiquated air force and its subsequent reliance on missiles for deterrence and defence. Technically, however, such procurement should be transacted through the Procurement Channel, and it is unclear how such non-compliance should be viewed. This exposes one shortcoming of the mechanism as it currently stands: the consequences of a violation are unclear.

There was originally no guidance on how to treat items simultaneously falling under NSG and MTCR controls; it was only clarified with time. Iran's ballistic-missile programme is not covered by the JCPOA, and UNSCR 2231 introduced a measure of ambiguity into how this issue will be policed (see Chapter Three). The resolution changed the approach on missile-related transfers to Iran from a complete prohibition to allowing states to engage in such transfers if they are approved by the Security Council on a case-by-case basis – an important distinction. As a practical matter, such permission is exceedingly unlikely, given Security Council dynamics and the veto power wielded by countries such as the US. But it is not at all clear how Iranian procurement without such approval is to be treated. According to various reports, Iran's procurement activity in this area appears to continue largely unchanged, without provoking much in the way of a response from the international community.[33]

It is also possible that innocuous purchases of dual-use items could unwittingly take place outside of the Procurement Channel. Although such an attempt would technically be inconsistent with Iran's commitment to use the Procurement Channel, it would presumably not be treated with the same severity as a deliberate attempt to buy sensitive items for use in Iran's nuclear programme covertly. It is not typically incumbent upon the importer to know the control status of goods, and lapses of this kind happen often enough even between established partners with mature compliance programmes. On the other hand, Iran could well claim ignorance in the hope that such activities would go unpunished. It is also possible, though somewhat less credible, that factions within Iran, such as the Islamic Revolutionary Guard Corps (IRGC), could use such activities to undermine the government of President Hassan Rouhani, which under the JCPOA is the ultimate guarantor that sensitive items are not diverted into illicit use.

Dispute-resolution process and possible responses

Paragraph 6.6 of Annex IV of the JCPOA establishes that 'any JCPOA participant may refer a procurement-related activity to the Joint Commission under the dispute-settlement mechanism if it is concerned that such activity is inconsistent with this JCPOA'.[34] Although this does not technically provide a mechanism for those countries not party to the JCPOA, as a practical matter they would be able to raise the issue in other contexts – with the IAEA, the Security Council or through a *note verbale* to a Joint Commission representative. The consideration would then enter the formal JCPOA dispute-resolution mechanism, which stipulates that if any party to the agreement believes that JCPOA commitments are not being met, it can refer the issue to the Joint Commission. The Joint Commission then has 15 days – or more, if this time period is extended by consensus – to resolve it. If no solution is found, any participant can refer the case to the ministers of foreign affairs from JCPOA participant countries, who have an additional 15 days – or more, if again extended by consensus – to consider it.

Alongside or instead of the ministerial review – though after consideration by the Joint Commission – the complaining party or the party whose performance is in question can request consideration by an Advisory Board, consisting of two members appointed by the participants to the dispute – one each – and an independent member. The Advisory Board will also have 15 days to consider the case and issue a non-binding opinion. If no solution is found, the Joint Commission will have an additional five days to consider the board's opinion and resolve the issue. If that is still not possible, and non-performance is deemed significant by the complaining party, that participant may cease honouring its commitments under the JCPOA either in whole or in part, and/or notify the UN Security Council. The Security Council will have 30 days to vote on a resolution to continue the waiving of sanctions. If this resolution is not adopted within this period, measures outlined in previous Security Council sanctions resolutions will be reimposed, restoring the entire sanctions architecture as it was before Implementation Day – the sanctions snap-back.

Sanctions snap-back would be one of the more extreme possible responses. Intermediate steps, however, are not at all clear. One possible response to a Procurement Channel violation is outlined in Annex B of UNSCR 2231, which states that the UN Security Council retains the ability to impose sanctions on individuals and entities for having

> engaged in, directly associated with or provided support for Iran's proliferation-sensitive nuclear activities undertaken contrary to Iran's commitments in the JCPOA or the development of nuclear weapon delivery systems, including through the involvement in procurement of prohibited items, goods, equipment, materials and technology specified in this statement.[35]

But there is no prescription for dealing with less egregious cases, which makes the deterrence aspect of the Procurement Channel slightly less credible. For such non-major offences, some experts have suggested measures such as slowing down or halting approvals in the Procurement Channel, reducing civil-nuclear cooperation or, if violations persist, reimposing some previously lifted sanctions.[36] A degree of flexibility is understandably required, but a discussion about these intermediate steps should at least take place among the P5+1 to develop a credible suite of options to respond to any questionable procurement activity.

The apparent lack of an effective investigative body poses obstacles to successful dispute resolution. In the case of recent allegations, it is unclear whether they were raised in the Joint Commission. By June 2018, the US was no longer a party to the JCPOA; the UAE, although in principle able to raise the issue through a third party, does not appear to have done so. Instead, both Emirati and US authorities engaged with the UN Secretariat, which, in accordance with its mandate, formally reported the allegations. Given the Secretariat's limited investigative remit, however, it has little authority to adjudicate such allegations.

The Panel of Experts – in theory set up as an independent body outside of the formal UN system – saw its independence challenged by the politics of the Security Council. The UN Secretariat's complete lack of such independence puts it in a much weaker position. Indeed, when it took on the role of supporting the implementation of UNSCR 2231, it was not initially clear that it would even retain the Panel's investigative responsibilities. This mandate was eventually established but its boundaries remain unclear. It seems plausible that the six allegations outlined in the June 2018 report will remain on the agenda for the foreseeable future, without any definitive judgement for or against Iran. In its response to the allegations, Iran stated that it is 'the responsibility of the exporting State to seek approval through the procurement channel'.[37] While this argument is, as a practical matter, not entirely unreasonable (it is difficult, if not impossible, for a state to control all trade originating in its territory), in accepting the mechanism Iran also accepted its own accountability for abiding by it. Without an independent body able to make definitive judgements, however, this accountability may not be established anytime soon – nor will Iran have a credible route to prove its innocence.

National governments will need to remain vigilant for any procurement-related activity that may seem suspicious. In this context, raising awareness of both the Procurement Channel and the remaining restrictions on Iran will be crucial, particularly in the private sector. In one example, a report by the Institute for Science and International Security suggested that sometime in the first half-year after Implementation Day, the AEOI sought to purchase carbon fibre from abroad, which was denied by the supplier and its government.[38] This is not necessarily an indication of any malfeasance on the part of Iran: because the transaction was denied by the supplier, it is unclear whether it would have been submitted to the Procurement Channel, and whether it would have been approved or denied. But it seems reasonable to assume that the purchase request was not turned down capriciously. If any potentially questionable activity is detected by national governments, it stands to reason that P5+1 governments would benefit from receiving this information. To be sure, it does not need to be made public: a discussion within the Joint Commission, or even informal sharing of information among partner countries, should suffice.

Future of the JCPOA

The economic benefits of the nuclear agreement have thus far fallen short of Iran's expectations. Whether these expectations were justified or not is a separate matter: as Iran sees it, it has not been able to reap the benefits it was promised. It is certainly true that businesses have been slower to engage with Iran than many observers anticipated, for many of the same reasons that have hindered the Procurement Channel. Banks, in particular, have been hesitant. Exposure to US sanctions is a major consideration for top-tier banks, some of which have been severely penalised by US regulators in the past. But substandard banking practices in Iran are also a factor: money laundering and terrorist financing are areas of significant concern. Iran does not have a tradition of dealing with these issues and, as some suggest, does not really grasp just how important anti-money laundering/combatting the financing of terrorism (AML/CFT) measures are to Western financial institutions. Although Tehran has engaged with the intergovernmental Financial Action Task

Force (FATF) and begun addressing some of its concerns, much more needs to be done before major financial institutions will be willing to engage. Perhaps most important, however, is the uncertainty over the deal's future, which mounted with Trump's election and subsequent withdrawal of the US from the JCPOA in May 2018 and reimposition of nuclear-related sanctions on Iran.

Extending the Procurement Channel?

If the JCPOA survives long enough for the Procurement Channel to reach its expiration date of 18 October 2025, an extension of the Channel beyond that timeline might merit consideration. Such an extension is, in principle, possible: as stipulated in the final paragraph of Annex B of UNSCR 2231:

> The duration of the provisions in this statement may be reviewed by the Joint Commission at the request of any participant at its biannual ministerial-level meetings, at which time the Joint Commission could make recommendations by consensus to the Security Council.

From a Western perspective, such an extension would have obvious benefits, allowing continued control over Iran's sensitive procurement and providing another window into its nuclear activities. The cost required to keep the mechanism running would likely be seen as a justifiable expense.

Iran, of course, would be far less enthusiastic about an extension. With the Procurement Channel in place, the Iranian government assumes responsibility and can be held accountable for any diversions from stated end uses. More importantly, the mechanism imposes a set of restrictions on Iran that do not apply to any other country – a proposition that Iran is vehemently opposed to as a matter of principle. Iran is very unlikely to engage in discussions on the subject in the current political environment, but the idea should not be dismissed out of hand, since the continued operation of the Procurement Channel would have some clear benefits for Tehran as well.

Aside from monitoring Iran's activities, the Procurement Channel was designed as a mechanism to 'rehabilitate' Iran after decades of illicit procurement. It is not an easy task, and the continued reluctance of companies to do business with Iran suggests that it may require more than a decade, as originally envisaged. The Channel also provides a degree of reassurance to companies, offering a sort of 'seal of approval' that their business with Iran is legitimate. In that, transactions submitted through the Procurement Channel benefit from what could be termed a 'presumption of approval', even though, of course, this is not absolute. It is a mechanism based on consensus, in which at least some parties are sympathetic to Iran, and one that the remaining parties to the JCPOA are determined to make work. The Procurement Channel benefits from a degree of political cover. It also provides Iran with an appeal process of sorts, one that is somewhat less discretionary than would normally be the case with national export-licensing bodies.

All this hinges on the assumption that Iran wants to rehabilitate itself, and that it wants continued access to Western-made goods. In principle, with only limited exceptions, Iran should be able to procure most of the nuclear-relevant goods it needs from countries such as China and Russia. They have reasonably strong manufacturing bases and are traditionally more lenient in controlling exports of sensitive goods. However, Iran has shown a clear preference for Western-made items. With the channel in place, it would be easier for Tehran to obtain them.

Conclusion and recommendations

Despite the relatively low level of activity in the Procurement Channel to date, the mechanism appears to be working. A reasonable number of transactions have been processed in the past two years, and the growing numbers seem to be a good sign for its future functioning – if the JCPOA survives. Some of the issues hindering its implementation are likely to be lessened with time; addressing others will require a concerted effort. Chief among them is raising awareness of the Procurement Channel and its procedures. It is an unprecedented and complex mechanism. As its implementation to date suggests, primarily countries with well-developed and efficient national export-control regimes have been meaningfully engaged with the Channel. In many other countries, however, even those with a relevant industrial base, awareness of it is limited or simply non-existent. To address this issue, increased outreach is crucial. At the same time, however, the bodies best positioned to conduct outreach, such as the UN Secretariat and the Procurement Working Group, do not have at their disposal the resources to do so. This situation is in urgent need of attention.

Recent allegations of transfers outside the Procurement Channel also raise concerns – not least about the apparent lack of a credible mechanism to resolve them. The UN Secretariat should be empowered to effectively monitor and investigate Iran's implementation of its nuclear-related commitments instead of simply reporting on the allegations it receives. Without a credible investigative capability, resolving any disputes over Iran's procurement will be difficult, with allegations lingering indefinitely. This risks souring the atmosphere around the Procurement Channel, which would render it much less effective.

At times, political considerations may out of necessity overtake rigorous enforcement: this is inherent in the conduct of foreign policy. But national and international authorities must strike a careful balance in order not to compromise the credibility of the mechanism itself. For that reason, it is also important to develop a credible, and reasonably flexible, range of responses to any questionable procurement activity by Iran that would avoid a zero-sum approach but retain the credibility of the Procurement Channel.

All this, of course, hedges on the broader question of the JCPOA's future. From the standpoint of curbing Iran's illicit procurement, the continued implementation of the deal is key. Attempts to control Iran's procurement proved largely unsuccessful prior to the JCPOA's adoption, under what was arguably the most comprehensive sanctions regime ever imposed. There is little reason to believe that renewed sanctions would be any more successful in stopping illicit procurement if the nuclear agreement falls apart.

While one might hope that the Procurement Channel could be maintained as an independent mechanism if the rest of the JCPOA were to fall away, this is highly unlikely. Firstly, Iran would have no incentive to accept the intrusive end-user verification and other requirements of the Procurement Channel if these were not linked to the benefits of the accord, as this would entail restrictions not applied to any other state. Secondly, if the JCPOA falls apart and Iran stops implementing its nuclear commitments, one of the other parties may have little choice but to trigger the dispute-resolution process and, with it, the snapback of UN sanctions. This, in turn, would restore the previous resolutions which prohibit Iranian procurement of nuclear-related goods and thus obviate the essence of the Procurement Channel. In sum, without the JCPOA, the mechanism cannot survive. Its loss, and the ensuing resumption of illicit nuclear trafficking by Iran, would be an unintended consequence of Trump's withdrawal from the deal.

CHAPTER THREE

Evaluating design intent in Iran's ballistic-missile programme[1]

Michael Elleman and Mark Fitzpatrick

Introduction

Many countries view Iran's robust ballistic-missile programme with concern – both near neighbours and states further afield. While neighbouring states have reason to worry about adversaries' missiles regardless of their payload, it is their potential ability to deliver nuclear weapons that causes most concern. If Iran did develop nuclear weapons, it would be Iran's missiles that would make them a potent deterrent. The decision by negotiators of the Joint Comprehensive Plan of Action (JCPOA) to limit the agreement to covering capabilities for producing nuclear warheads, and not to cover the means of delivering such weapons, is one of the major criticisms levelled against the deal. As noted in Chapter One, when China, Russia and Iran blocked an effort to include limitations on missile development in the deal, the Obama administration justified the exclusion on grounds that delivery mechanisms were less important if Iran were blocked from obtaining nuclear weapons to begin with. The limits agreed in the JCPOA on enrichment capability will expire by 2031, however, which will theoretically enable Iran to produce sufficient highly enriched uranium (HEU) for a nuclear weapon in a matter of days; possessing well developed ballistic missiles capable of delivering such weapons would then be highly significant.

Curbing Iran's missile programme is a top priority for the United States' current administration. On 12 January 2018, President Donald Trump demanded that European parties to the JCPOA work with the US to 'fix' the deal. He called for Congress to pass legislation that would explicitly state that 'long-range missile and nuclear weapons programmes are inseparable, and that Iran's development and testing of missiles should be subject to severe sanctions'.[2] A slower pace in missile testing since mid-2016 – Iran launched only two medium-range ballistic missiles (MRBMs) in 2017 and none so far since at least July that year – does not appear to have reduced the attention that the Trump administration and other critics of the JCPOA have focused on the missile issue.

It is often assumed that Iran's ballistic missiles have little purpose other than to be mated with future nuclear weapons. Yet this assumption has not been subject to rigorous technical analysis, and critics have often failed to differentiate between Iran's various missile systems. This chapter examines whether and to what extent Iran's missiles are 'designed to be capable of delivering nuclear weapons', to employ the language of the relevant United Nations Security Council resolution, as described below.

International legal frameworks for ballistic missiles

UNSCR 2231
Some critics of the JCPOA claim that Iran's missile tests 'violate' the provisions of UN Security Council Resolution 2231, which was adopted on 20 July 2015 in order to endorse the JCPOA (concluded six days earlier) and to bring UN mandates into

alignment with the agreement. Unlike the JCPOA, this resolution does cover Iran's ballistic missiles. It states that:

> Iran is called upon not to undertake any activity related to ballistic missiles designed to be capable of delivering nuclear weapons, including launches using such ballistic missile technology, until the date eight years after the JCPOA Adoption Day or until the date on which the IAEA submits a report confirming the Broader Conclusion, whichever is earlier.[3]

The language differs in three key ways from that used in the previous resolution applying to Iran's missiles, UNSCR 1929 (2010). Each reflects a compromise made by Western powers in order to retain restrictions on ballistic missiles in the resolution. The first of these is the reference to a limited time duration. In the final stages of negotiations, Iran, supported by China and Russia, had demanded that the accompanying Security Council resolution – which would supersede all previous resolutions on Iran's nuclear programme – remove all restrictions applying to missiles. Secondly, rather than saying the Security Council 'decides that Iran shall not undertake' any ballistic-missile-related activity, UNSCR 2231 only 'call[s] upon' Iran not to do so. Thirdly, whereas UNSCR 1929 prohibited activity related to ballistic missiles 'capable of delivering nuclear weapons', the 2015 resolution added the qualifier 'designed to be capable of delivering' such weapons, raising the issue of how to judge intent.

Most concerned states judge that because the operative verb 'calls upon' does not carry the same force as 'decides', missile tests after 18 October 2015 (JCPOA Adoption Day) are not a violation of UNSCR 2231. While a legal case possibly could be made that the restriction is nevertheless legally binding, the language is generally understood to be hortatory. In practice, most states have refrained from calling tests conducted after the adoption of UNSCR 2231 a violation. France, Germany, the United Kingdom and the US typically characterise Iran's missile tests as being 'in defiance of' or 'inconsistent with' the resolution.

The insertion of 'designed to' aimed to address the intended purpose of the missiles in question, a change that Iran demanded for vindicatory purposes. As former US State Department official Greg Thielmann puts it, adding that phrase 'implies nuclear weapons intent must now be established in assessing the design of any missile launched by Iran – an even higher bar in light of Iran's acceptance of stringent limits on its nuclear program'.[4] Intent is difficult to assess objectively, but reasonable answers can be reached by drawing on intelligence findings and forensic evidence.

Neither UNSCR 2231 nor its predecessor resolutions define any of the terms in the phrase 'designed to be capable of delivering nuclear weapons'. Nor are they defined in any other binding international instrument. Even the term 'nuclear weapon' remains largely undefined: the Non-Proliferation Treaty (NPT), signed in 1968, casts as wide a net as possible, regularly using the phrase 'nuclear weapons or other nuclear explosive devices' as the subject of its injunctions.[5] It is worth considering some of the international frameworks that attempt to define missiles' nuclear capability (or lack thereof).

Missile Technology Control Regime standards

The Missile Technology Control Regime (MTCR) is an informal and voluntary arrangement, now among 35 states, established in 1987 to curb the spread of unmanned delivery systems for nuclear weapons and, later, other weapons of mass destruction (WMD). Early on, the MTCR set guidelines which called for a 'strong presumption of denial' of exports of technologies and hardware for missiles and other unmanned platforms capable of delivering a payload exceeding 500 kilograms to a distance exceeding 300 kilometres.

Western government officials contend that any Iranian missiles with this payload and range capability are 'inherently capable of delivering nuclear weapons', and that their testing therefore defies UNSCR 2231. A joint letter from France, Germany, the United Kingdom and the United States to the president of the UN Security Council in March 2016 used this language in condemning Iran's launch of five ballistic missiles on 8–9 March, including a *Ghadr* missile that flew 1,400 km.[6] On 7 February 2017, the four states similarly contended that a *Khorramshahr* missile that Iran had test-fired on 29 January was 'inherently capable of delivering nuclear weapons'.[7] The logic here is that any systems that exceed the 300 km/500 kg threshold were designed to be capable of carrying nuclear weapons. In criticising the *Simorgh* space-launch vehicle that Iran launched on 27 July 2017, the four countries said in a letter to the UN secretary-general dated 2 August that if configured as a ballistic missile, the rocket was 'inherently capable of delivering nuclear weapons'.[8]

There is no disagreement between Security Council members that missiles above the 300 km/500 kg threshold are inherently capable of carrying nuclear weapons. Disagreement emerges, however, on the issue of intent, and whether specific missile systems are designed for nuclear-weapons delivery.

On 16 August 2017, Russia's representative to the UN addressed a letter to the secretary-general taking issue with the claim by the four Western powers, stating that there was no evidence that Iranian ballistic missiles were specifically designed to carry nuclear weapons. China agreed with Russia's position that UNSCR 2231 set an intent-based standard, and that there was no proof of intent to deliver nuclear weapons with these systems. The argument by Russia, China and Iran therefore rests on lack of evidence, although their logic is stronger in the case of space-launch vehicles, which are not specifically designed to be ballistic missiles. Iran's ambassador to the UN followed up with a letter on 23 August 2017, stating that the MTCR threshold was not an internationally agreed definition and that the 'technical characteristics and operational requirements of the satellite launch vehicles clearly make them distinct from ballistic missile systems'.[9] The test launch therefore could not be seen as inconsistent with the resolution, Iran's ambassador argued.

It is worth dwelling on the reasoning behind the MTCR threshold. These 'Category I' parameters were set because 500 kg is at the low end of the mass of a first-generation nuclear weapon, and 300 km was deemed to be the strategic distance in the most compact theatres in which nuclear weapons might be used.[10] According to Richard H. Speier, the US Department of Defense policy official who spearheaded the MTCR negotiations in the mid-1980s:

> The 300 kilometer range figure was derived by inspection of the Korean theater, the most compact theater to which 'nuclear capable missiles' might be expected to proliferate. The 'minimum range likely to be interesting to local strategic planners' in that theater – taking account of the desire to site missiles well back from the DMZ and to be able to strike targets well beyond the DMZ – appears to be about 300 kilometers.[11]

It may not have been solely a coincidence that 300 km was also the range of the Soviet *Scud*-B systems that were being widely exported at the time, to the consternation of the US and its allies. The threshold decided upon was well above the capability of the Soviet *Scud*-A, which had a range of 150 km when carrying a nuclear warhead. By 1987, however, that system had long been out of service and was not a proliferation concern. Moreover, setting a range limit as low as 150 km would have captured some US systems, particularly the MGM-52 *Lance* – a dual-use tactical missile that was exported to NATO allies and Israel.[12] A 150 km limit would also have included tactical artillery systems that are widely used and exported by the major powers, such as the US MGM-140A ATACMS and the Soviet/Russian OTR-21 *Tochka* (SS-21 *Scarab*) rockets. When Russia joined the MTCR in 1995, it had to swallow the 500 kg/300 km parameter.[13]

Although non-binding, the MTCR guidelines offer the only international standard available for ballistic missiles. The guidelines call on all states to adhere 'in the interest of inter-national peace and security'. The 300 km/500 kg threshold has subsequently been widely used in various international and national export-control programmes. The sanctions imposed by the UN Panel of Experts on Iran, for example, informally adopted the MTCR parameters for practical purposes, without the panel's reports explicitly saying so.[14] It should be empha-sised, however, that the MTCR is not a treaty, and is not legally binding even for its members (unless they have passed national legislation making it so) – much less for Iran and the other 160-odd states that are not members.

The MTCR limit should be considered an upper bound. More sophisticated nuclear weapons can weigh considerably less: the W80, for instance, a small thermonuclear warhead that the US began producing in 1979 for delivery by cruise missiles, weighs just 130 kg. It should also be noted that new guide-lines adopted by the MTCR in 1993 call for a restriction on the sale to countries of any missile or unmanned aircraft thought to be intended for delivering what it called 'weapons of mass destruction'. This new restriction therefore added an element of intent to guidelines that previously only considered capability. While the new criterion was added to address chemical and biological weapons, which typically weigh much less than 500 kg, expanding the guidelines to cover all WMD also implicitly covered miniaturised nuclear weapons. Other complete delivery systems that have a range equal to or greater than 300 km, regardless of payload size, are also covered by Category II, Item 19, of the MTCR guidelines, under which members agree to exercise restraint but have greater flexibility in the treatment of transfer applications.[15]

The Hague Code of Conduct against Ballistic Missile Proliferation and the Proliferation Security Initiative

There are two other international arrangements which seek to limit missile proliferation. The 2002 Hague Code of Conduct against Ballistic Missile Proliferation (HCoC, also known as the International Code of Conduct against Ballistic Missile Proliferation) codifies the MTCR principle that governments have an obligation to combat the spread of ballistic-missile technology. The 138 signing states (as of 2017) pledge not to aid ballistic-missile proliferation, although it is a political arrangement, rather than a binding commitment. Iran and 12 other states in the Middle East, including Egypt, Israel, Saudi Arabia and the United Arab Emirates, have not signed the HCoC.

The Proliferation Security Initiative (PSI), established in 2003, is a loose US-led coalition of states that have agreed to cooperate in interdicting shipments of WMD and related materials, including the export of missiles to terrorists and countries of proliferation concern. As of 2015, 105 states had signed the PSI statement of interdiction principles, which commits participants 'to establish a more coordinated and effective basis through which to impede and stop shipments of WMD, delivery systems, and related materials flowing to and from states and non-state actors of proliferation concern'.[16] The statement does not name the countries of concern, but in practice, they have been Iran and North Korea. As they do not impose MTCR-like guidelines, nor indeed any limits, the HCoC and PSI are of less relevance for assessing the nuclear capabilities of Iran's missiles. Like the MTCR, however, both arrangements provide policy tools for concerned states that seek to curtail Iran's ballistic-missile programmes. The significant number of signatories to both can also be seen to provide a greater sense of international legitimacy than the MTCR, which non-member states often characterise as a cartel.[17]

UNSCR 2231 trade bans

Three other elements of UNSCR 2231 are particularly relevant to Iran's ballistic-missile programme. Firstly, the resolution stipulates that the supply to Iran of all items, materials, equipment, goods and technology and related material, and training or services which the state wishing to sell such goods 'determines could contribute to the development of nuclear weapon development systems' is allowed only on a case-by-case basis by the Security Council. This provision (Annex B, paragraph 4), which amounts to a missile-export ban to Iran, will be lifted eight years after JCPOA Adoption Day – that is, on 18 October 2023 – or after the International Atomic Energy Agency (IAEA) submits a report confirming the broader conclusion, whichever is earlier.

Secondly, the supply to Iran of major pieces of military equipment, including 'missiles or missile systems', is also allowed only on a case-by-case basis by the Security Council. This provision (Annex B, paragraph 5), which is in essence an arms-export ban, will expire in 2020, or when the broader conclusion is confirmed. It should be noted that, unlike paragraph 4, this section does not use the words 'nuclear weapons delivery systems'. This suggests a further need for concerned states to differentiate between missiles that were designed to be nuclear-capable and those for which this might not be the case.

Thirdly, all states are obligated to prevent the transfer of arms from Iran by their nationals, with the same five-year duration applicable. This clause (Annex B, paragraph 6b) also prohibits Iranian arms exports, as the first paragraph of the annex sets out that 'all States' throughout the resolution refers to 'all States without exception'. Technically, Iran is required to 'take the necessary measures to prevent' itself from engaging in arms exports. When debris from a rocket fired by Houthi rebels in Yemen at King Khalid International Airport in Riyadh, Saudi Arabia, on 4 November 2017 indicated that the weapon was derived from the *Qiam* missile made in Iran, US Ambassador to the UN Nikki Haley cited the incident as a violation of the arms-export bans imposed by UNSCR 2231 and UNSCR 2216 – the Security Council adopted the latter, which bans arms sales to Yemen, in April 2015. Iran denied that it had supplied the missile or, indeed, that it had provided the Houthis with any weapons at all.[18] A January 2018 report by a UN Panel of Experts reportedly concluded that Iran had indeed violated the Yemen arms embargo by failing to prevent Houthi rebels from obtaining Iranian missiles, although the panel did not explicitly conclude that Iran had supplied the missiles.[19]

Iran's ballistic-missile programme

Motivations
If states and policymakers are to consider intent under UNSCR 2231, it is important to understand why Iran acquired ballistic missiles, and why its programme evolved to become the largest and most diverse in the Middle East (although it

is not the most lethal, nor do Iran's missiles have the longest range).[20] Under the Shah, Iran had the largest air force in the Gulf, including more than 400 combat planes. Soon after the 1979 Iranian Revolution and the subsequent break in ties with the West, Iran's deep-strike capability rapidly degraded because the country no longer had access to the spare parts, maintenance, pilot training and advanced armaments that the US had supplied prior to the 1979 revolution. With its air force rendered incapable of responding to Iraq's attacks on Iranian cities in the early years of the Iran–Iraq War (1980–88), Tehran turned to Libya to procure *Scud*-B missiles to deal with an immediate wartime need. In March 1985, Iran retaliated against Iraq with its limited stock of *Scud*-Bs for the first time. The attacks shocked the Iraqi regime and large portions of its populace, which until that time had been isolated from the war's violence. Then-president of Iraq Saddam Hussein promptly agreed to suspend missile fire against Iranian cities if Tehran demonstrated similar restraint.

From Iran's perspective, ballistic missiles played a critical role in responding to Iraq's air and missile strikes against its cities and economic infrastructure. The apparent success of Iran's retaliatory strikes set off a scramble to procure more missiles for use against Iraq, and led Tehran to establish programmes aimed at developing the industrial infrastructure and technical know-how that would allow it to produce missiles and rockets domestically.

Despite the procurement of additional *Scud*-B missiles from Syria and North Korea soon after the initial use of the missiles, and Iran's readiness to fire them when necessary, air and missile strikes by Iraq resumed in the latter years of the war, marked by the 'war of the cities', during which each side pummelled the other's urban centres. While Iran's newly acquired missiles failed to deter Iraq, a quarter of Tehran's residents fled as Iraqi *al*

Hussein missiles, widely rumoured to be equipped with chemical warheads, rained down on the city. The attacks on Tehran left an indelible mark on Iran's elite, cementing a belief that missiles are a formidable strategic tool. The regime therefore prioritised the procurement from North Korea of additional *Scud*-Bs, and *Scud*-Cs (which have a 500 km range), and the building of the infrastructure and technical foundations of an indigenous programme to develop and produce missiles. Iran renamed the *Scud*-B and -C missiles, respectively, the *Shahab*-1 and *Shahab*-2.

The priority Iran assigns to ballistic missiles is reflected by the size and scope of its inventory. The contents of Iran's stockpile are summarised in Table 1.

The First Gulf War (1990–91) and the US-led invasion of Iraq in 2003 further convinced Tehran of the importance of ballistic missiles. The regime witnessed how quickly the US-led coalition devastated the Iraqi army in 1991, which had battled Iran to a standstill during an eight-year war. The only notable response from Iraq during *Operation Desert Storm* came in the form of 88 *Scud*-type missile attacks against Israel, Saudi Arabia and other Gulf countries. While the missile strikes on Israel did not fracture the international coalition aligned against Iraq, the diversion of coalition aircraft to the '*Scud*-hunting mission', and away from the assault on Iraqi troops and equipment, reinforced Tehran's belief that missiles have strategic value beyond the actual damage they inflict.

Development

Considering missiles to be essential to both deterrence and defence, Tehran steadily expanded its missile arsenal throughout the 1990s and thereafter. It invested heavily in domestic industries and infrastructure to lessen its dependence on unreliable foreign sources. Iran also sought to extend

Table 1 **Iran's ballistic-missile capabilities**

Missile	Range	Payload	Fuel	Numbers	Mission/ intended targets	Note
Fateh-110	200–225 km	450 kg	Solid	100+	Battlefield	Guided
Khalij Fars	200–225 km	450 kg	Solid	<50?	Anti-ship	Limited capability
Hormuz-1/-2	200–225 km	450 kg	Solid	<50?	Anti-radar	Limited capability
Fateh-313	300–325 km	350 kg	Solid	?	Battlefield?	New
Zulfiqar	300–350 km?	350 kg	Solid	?	Battlefield?	New
Shahab-1	300 km	1,000 kg	Liquid		Airfields, military bases	Scud-B
Shahab-2	500 km	720 kg	Liquid	200–300	Airfields, military bases	Scud-C
Qiam	~700 km	500 kg	Liquid		Airfields, military bases	Modified Scud-C
Shahab-3	800–1,000 km	~1,000 kg	Liquid		Strategic	Nodong
Ghadr	1,600 km	700 kg	Liquid	~ 100	Strategic	Modified Nodong
Emad	1,600 km	700 kg	Liquid		Strategic	Modified Ghadr
Sajjil	2,000 km	700 kg	Solid	18?	Strategic	Deployed?
Khorramshahr	2,000 km	~ 1,200 kg	Liquid	Under development	Strategic	Musudan?

The missiles highlighted in bold exceed the Missile Technology Control Regime's thresholds of 300 km range, 500 kg payload, and can be considered to be capable of delivering a nuclear warhead.

its reach by procuring *Nodong* missiles from North Korea in the mid-1990s, which it renamed the *Shabab-3*. Initial test launches in 1998 made it clear, however, that the *Shahab-3*'s maximum range of 1,000 km fell short of Tehran's goal of threatening targets in Israel, unless the missiles were launched from Iran's border with Iraq, where the firing crews would be vulnerable to pre-launch strikes. The presence of the US military in Iraq after the overthrow of Saddam in 2003 accelerated Tehran's efforts to perfect a new system that could reach Israel when launched from positions deep inside Iran's interior.

In overhauling the *Shahab*-3, Iran created the *Ghadr* system (sometimes transliterated as *Qadr*), which possesses a range of 1,600 km. It is constructed using an aluminium alloy, instead of steel (used for the *Shahab*-3). The *Ghadr*'s propellant tanks were extended to carry additional fuel, and the missile's maximum payload mass is 400–500 kg less than that of the *Shahab*-3. These modifications almost double the achievable range, so the *Ghadr* can be usefully defined as a new missile. Iran carried out the first test flight of the *Ghadr* in 2004, and issued the missile to military units three or four years later.

In a parallel effort, Iran leveraged its experience of indigenously producing a family of solid-fuelled, heavy-artillery rockets to develop and flight-test the two-stage, solid-propellant *Sajjil* missile. After almost a decade of work, Iran began flight trials of the *Sajjil*, which has a range of 2,000 km, in 2008, but abruptly halted testing in early 2011, before development was complete. It is unclear why Iran suspended the flight-test programme, though intractable technical challenges – possibly related to Iran's inability to consistently source high-quality ingredients for production of large, solid-fuel motors in the face of sanctions and export controls – seem the most likely explanation.[21]

The putative issues that appear to have beleaguered the development of the *Sajjil* MRBM have not deterred Iran from constructing facilities near Shahrud to support the manu-facture of large, solid-fuel motors.[22] The size of the facilities is consistent with low-rate production, suggesting that the motors will be used to boost satellites into orbit, though the site could be expanded quickly to increase throughput. Exploiting the facility to manufacture large motors for an intercontinental ballistic missile (ICBM) programme cannot be dismissed, though a fully developed, operationally reliable solid-fuel missile capable of reaching the US homeland would likely require a decade of effort, and multiple test flights in a ballistic-missile mode. Activities at the Shahrud site nevertheless warrant close monitoring.

Iran recently unveiled another ballistic missile with a similar range. On 22 September 2017, Iran revealed the *Khorramshahr* during a military parade; it was first flight-tested that January. The missile has a diameter of 1.5 metres, and is about 13.5 m in length. It appears to be based on the North Korean *Musudan* (*Hwasong*-10) missile, although it possesses a much larger nosecone. Media reports indicate that there have been two abortive flight tests of the *Khorramshahr*.[23] During a first test launch on 11 July 2016, the missile reportedly exploded shortly after lift-off, much like North Korea's failed attempts with the *Musudan* in spring of the same year. The second test attempt, on 29 January 2017, is said to have failed catastrophically during the unpowered phase of its flight, about 900 km from the launch site. It is unclear why it failed long after the engine had been shut down, and before it would have re-entered the atmosphere. Assuming it is powered by the same engine as the *Musudan*, an engineering reconstruction of the *Khorramshahr* indicates it has a maximum range of 2,000–2,200 km when carrying a 1,000 kg payload.

Adding another note of concern, the US Treasury in 2016 asserted that Iran and North Korea were working together on development of an '80-ton booster'.[24] It is unclear if the description refers to a booster (or stage) of this weight, or an engine capable of generating this amount of thrust. The latter is consistent with the two-chamber engine that propels the first stage of North Korea's *Hwasong*-15 ICBM. If Iran possessed a handful of these large engines – though there is no independent evidence that it does – Tehran could break out and test a long-range missile at a time of its choosing, much as North Korea did in 2017.

With the development and deployment of medium-range systems, Iran can credibly threaten to strike its regional rivals, including Israel and Saudi Arabia. However, the poor accuracy of Iran's most advanced missile systems limits their military utility. Iran's *Shahab*-1 missiles, for instance, carry one-tonne high-explosive warheads, which when detonated have a lethal radius of 30–70 m, depending on the vulnerability of the target, and have a circular error probable (CEP) of around 800–1,000 m. CEP is defined as the radius of a circle within which one-half of the warheads are expected to land. As its warheads land on average 800–1,000 m from their targets, and its lethal effects extend to less than 70 m, the *Shahab*-1 has a mission-success probability of between 0.1% and 1% for a soft target, such as unprotected humans or exposed aircraft. For hardened targets, the probability drops to as low as 0.01%.[25] From the perspective of military planners, to destroy with moderate confidence a single, fixed-point military target, Iran would have to allocate a very significant percentage, if not all, of its missile inventory to one specific mission.

Against large military targets, such as an airfield or seaport, Iran could conduct harassment attacks aimed at disrupting operations or causing damage, but its missiles are not capable of halting critical military activities. Missile defences arrayed across the Arabian Peninsula, Israel and Turkey further attenuate the disruptive effects of Iranian missile assaults on military facilities. Given these constraints on military effectiveness, Iran has historically viewed its missile arsenal as a tool for deterring attack by threatening to punish an adversary's population and civilian infrastructure, as it did during the Iran–Iraq War. Iran's threats extend to US partners in the Gulf region, especially those which might support US military operations against Iran.

Nuclear hedging

In contrast to the limited military utility of conventionally armed missiles, nuclear payloads have a lethal radius measured in kilometres. The compact size and massive destructive power of nuclear warheads make them ideal for use on ballistic missiles, even those that are inaccurate. While Iran insists that its missile systems are 'defensive, conventional and deterrent' in nature, it stands to reason that Iran would at least examine the possibility of arming its missiles with a nuclear weapon.[26] Indeed, there is evidence that some of its missile systems have also been designed to carry a nuclear payload.

Information smuggled out of Iran suggests that Tehran pursued a study aimed at arming the *Shahab*-3 with nuclear warheads. According to US officials, in early 2004, an Iranian defector turned over to Western intelligence officials a laptop – reportedly taken without the knowledge of its owner – which contained thousands of documents relating to an alleged nuclear-weapons-development effort. Among the documents were schematics for Iran's *Shahab*-3 showing efforts in 2002–03 to fit a spherical object with the characteristics of a nuclear-implosion weapon into the missile's conical nosecone, and designed to detonate at an altitude of 600 m.[27] This was the detonation altitude of the atomic bomb at Hiroshima.[28] Other documents on the laptop contained scientific notes highly suggestive of triggers to compress HEU spheres into a critical mass for a nuclear explosion, as well as drawings for a 400 m-deep shaft that appeared designed for an underground nuclear test.[29]

Iran maintains that the documents were forged, but British, French and German intelligence agencies with which the US shared the information all agreed they appeared authentic.[30] The IAEA in February 2010 assessed that information it had received about Iran's alleged weapons studies was broadly consistent and credible in terms of the technical detail, the time frame in which the activities were conducted and the people and organizations involved. Altogether, this raises concerns about the possible existence in Iran of past or current undisclosed activities related to the development of a nuclear payload for a missile.[31]

On 30 April 2018, Israeli Prime Minister Benjamin Netanyahu unveiled documents, drawings and computer files that he said Israeli agents had seized from a storage facility in Tehran in January of that year. Netanyahu described the documentation as a secret 'atomic archive' that provided proof of Iran's illicit nuclear-weapons programme. Among the more than 55,000 pages of documents and 183 CDs were drawings and descriptions of a nuclear-implosion device mounted inside a *Shahab*-3 nosecone. The nuclear bomb had an estimated diameter of 585 millimetres; the diameter of the nosecone that corresponds to the maximum width of the nuclear bomb was about 720 mm. The space between the nuclear device's outer surface and the nosecone's inner surface is needed to secure the bomb within the warhead and to insulate it from the heat and vibrational loads experienced during flight, including atmospheric re-entry.

The documentation reported to be contained on the laptop, and the information Netanyahu unveiled, suggest that Iran's presumptive nuclear-bomb design was intended for use on a *Shahab*-3 missile. The geometry of the *Shahab*-3's re-entry vehicle and the missile's flight-performance profile indicate that when loaded with a conventional weapon, it has a total mass of 1,200–1,300 kg, and can fly about 800–900 km.[32] The calculated high-explosive weapons mass would be in the order of 1,000 kg.

While it might seem reasonable to assess that the *Ghadr* missile system, being based on the *Shahab*-3, would also be intended for nuclear delivery, the geometry of its weapons bay suggests otherwise. The *Ghadr* employs a triconic nosecone that is designed to fit a warhead in its 600 mm diameter cylindrical section. This section is too small to house the nuclear-implosion device described in the documents Israeli intelligence smuggled out of Iran. It is reasonable to argue, therefore, that the *Ghadr* was designed to carry conventional warheads, not nuclear ones. This judgement also holds for the *Qiam* and *Sajjil*, which share the same triconic nosecone. This conclusion would need to be adjusted if Iran were able to develop or acquire designs for a smaller nuclear warhead.

Accuracy over range

Iranian decision-makers understand that the ability to punish potential foes and their supporters may not provide sufficient deterrence, especially given the myriad missile-defence systems deployed by Israel, the US and its partners in the Gulf. Consequently, Iran has spent the past decade reprioritising its missile-development efforts away from increasing the range of its systems and growing its stockpile of *Shahab*-type missiles, to focusing on enhancing the precision and lethality of missiles it hopes to develop in the future.

Iran's pursuit of greater precision is evidenced by the development of the *Fateh*-110 semi-guided rocket. There is no evidence that this system was ever intended to carry nuclear weapons, and its range/payload capability (maximum 250 km/350 kg) falls well short of the MTCR Category I threshold. Efforts to enhance accuracy began in the early 2000s, when Iranian engineers incorporated a simple navigation and guidance system, and four aerodynamic-control surfaces mounted just below the rocket's warhead section. The navigation unit, which senses deviations in the rocket's pitch and yaw, keeps the rocket on a preprogrammed orientation (i.e., angle of attack) during the boost and ascent phases of flight by adjusting the aerodynamic fins, thereby establishing a more consistent trajectory profile. The flight-stabilisation system significantly reduced the *Fateh-110*'s lateral dispersion. Range dispersion, while slightly improved, remained affected by inconsistencies in the rocket motor's performance.

While marking a significant improvement in accuracy, the first and second generations of the *Fateh-110* still lack the precision needed to reliably strike military targets. This was made clear during the *Great Prophet 7* military exercises in 2012, when Iranian forces unleashed a volley of *Fateh-110*s at a mock airfield, resulting in a spatial distribution of impact craters consistent with a CEP between 800 m and 1,100 m.[33]

Since 2012, Iranian engineers have likely worked to enhance the *Fateh-110*'s navigation, guidance and control system, so that it continuously corrects deviations along its full trajectory, including its final approach to the target. The missile would necessarily have to fly within the atmosphere to maintain positive-aerodynamic control over its entire path to the target, which limits the *Fateh-110*'s maximum range to roughly 200–250 km when carrying a 350 kg payload. In principle, future generations of the *Fateh-110* could be used to reliably destroy fixed-point targets. It is unclear how soon Iran will succeed in developing precision-guided, close-range missiles, although another five years of intense effort are likely needed. Iran's development of the *Fateh-110* family of missiles – which includes the optically guided, anti-ship *Khalij Fars* and the anti-radar *Hormuz* systems, as well as the *Fateh-313* – suggests that Iran seeks to produce and field highly accurate missiles capable of shaping the outcome of future military conflicts.

Iran flight-tested another variant of the *Fateh*-110 in September 2016. The *Zulfiqar* has the same dimensions as the *Fateh*-110, but Iranian sources claim that it has a range of 700–750 km when armed with a 500 kg warhead.[34] Such claims are likely gross exaggerations. Even if engineers replaced the metal motor casing with lighter composite materials, and employed a high-performance solid propellant, the *Zulfiqar* mock-up paraded could not hit targets at 500 km, let alone 700–750 km. A range of 300–350 km is more likely, although the warhead mass used at these distances would probably weigh less than 400 kg. In addition to this flight test, Iran reportedly used *Zulfiqar* missiles in operations in Syria in June 2017, when one *Qiam* and five or six *Zulfiqar* missiles were fired against a stronghold of the Islamic State, also known as ISIS or ISIL, in retaliation for terrorist attacks in Iran earlier that month.[35]

The test launch of the medium-range *Emad* missile in 2015 offers further evidence of Iran's desire to enhance missile accuracy. The *Emad* appears to be a *Ghadr* missile equipped with a new, separating warhead. Four small fins located at the base of the warhead section could potentially steer the warhead towards a target after re-entry. The principles, techniques and subsystems needed for effective manoeuvrability during descent through the atmosphere, however, are very different from those employed on the shorter-range *Fateh*-110. Iran is many years away from mastering the technologies required for a precision-guided, medium-range ballistic missile.

The prioritisation of improved precision over increased range – which began about a decade ago – marked a discernible shift in Iran's missile doctrine: away from one that relies solely on punishing would-be attackers by striking large, high-value targets like cities, to a strategy that aims also to deny potential foes their military objectives. This reorientation is consistent with wider shifts in Iran's overarching military doctrine, as encapsulated in the 'mosaic defence' strategy, which was formalised in 2007 when Supreme Leader Sayyid Ali Khamenei appointed Mohammad Ali Jafari commander of the Islamic Revolutionary Guard Corps (IRGC).[36] The mosaic defence doctrine establishes many strategic objectives, as well as three asymmetric, operational tactics to impede conventional military advances by an attacker: firstly, proxies provide a forward-based fighting force; secondly, guerrilla warfare at sea impedes a navy-supported invasion; and thirdly, the implicit threat of extraterritorial attacks with ballistic missiles deters adversaries. An arsenal of accurate, highly lethal ballistic missiles would support all three elements of Iran's asymmetric approach to warfare. Heavy-artillery rockets and short-range missiles, if they can deliver ordnance precisely, provide firepower to support proxy forces, constrain – though do not deny – an enemy's access to territory along Iran's borders, and raise the human and material cost of massing an invading army in a neighbouring country.

Iran argues that its missiles are strictly conventional. In July 2015, shortly after all parties had agreed to the JCPOA, Iran's foreign ministry said in a statement that Iran's ballistic missiles 'are strictly defensive and … have not been conceived to carry nuclear weapons', arguing that they were irrelevant to UNSCR 2231.[37] As evidence, Iranian officials insist that the country's missile-testing programme is focused on improving accuracy rather than on extending the range of missiles. In October 2017, Foreign Minister Javad Zarif claimed that Iran's missiles were 'now accurate to within seven meters', and that such accuracy 'would be entirely unnecessary for a nuclear payload'.[38] Iran also points to a fatwa issued by Khamenei in 2005 against the development, production, stockpiling and use of nuclear weapons as evidence of lack of nuclear intent.[39] Furthermore, in October 2017, Iranian officials began to refer to Khamenei's policy of limiting the range of missiles to 2,000 km.[40] Military command-ers noted, however, that Iran had the capacity to extend the range and would do so if Europe were to present a threat.[41]

Iran's claims are consistent with the direction of its missile programmes over the past half-dozen years, wherein devel-opment activities have focused almost entirely on improving the accuracy and military utility of its conventionally armed missiles. But Tehran's assertions that accuracy is unnecessary to deliver a nuclear payload are incorrect. Hardened targets, such as Israel's Dimona nuclear reactor, or deeply buried command-and-control bunkers, are reasonably immune to conventional warheads, even those that make a direct hit. For a missile warhead to successfully breach the reactor core at Dimona, or penetrate deeply enough into the earth to destroy under-ground facilities, a combination of precision and the power of a nuclear weapon are necessary. (Air-dropped mega conven-tional warheads such as the GBU-43/B Massive Ordnance Air Blast (MOAB) can accomplish such tasks, but are far too large for missile delivery.) During the later years of the Cold War, both the Soviet Union and the US prioritised the development of ICBMs capable of placing their warheads within 50 m of an intended target. Building an arsenal of precision-guided nuclear weapons was central to the counterforce strategy pursued by both Moscow and Washington. Iran is not pres-ently capable of developing missiles with the performance and reliability of the United States' *Trident* II or *Minuteman* systems, nor Russia's SS-18 or *Topol*-M systems, but Tehran's claims that highly accurate missiles are inconsistent with nuclear delivery are demonstrably untrue.

Nevertheless, it would be useful to lock in Iran's self-declared range limit through negotiations that made it a verifiable commitment. A limit of 2,000 km would mean that Iran's missiles posed little threat beyond the Middle East.

Although part of southeast Europe is within 2,000 km from the northwest tip of Iran, launch crews would need to fire any missiles from considerably further away from the border to make them less vulnerable to pre-emption. The US is 9,000 km away. Ensuring that Iran does not have an ICBM would put to rest the most alarmist concerns about its missile programme. As discussed below, however, a 2,000 km limit would mean forgoing the *Khorramshahr*, which can travel up to 2,800 km, depending on the mass of the payload. Iran would not likely accept such limits unless they also applied to other states in the Middle East. How such a multinational agreement might be achieved falls beyond the scope of this paper, but one of the authors has sketched out ideas elsewhere.[42]

Space-launch vehicles

There is no doubt that Iran's space-launch vehicle would be capable of delivering nuclear weapons if configured as ballistic missiles, with various modifications including a survivable re-entry vehicle. Iran's ambitious space programme potentially 'could serve as a test bed for developing ICBM technologies', according to the US National Air and Space Intelligence Center.[43] The programme also provides engineers with critical experience developing powerful booster rockets that could be used in developing longer-range missiles, including ICBMs. That said, labelling these development efforts an ICBM programme would be an overstatement.

Iran operates two satellite launchers: the *Safir* and the *Simorgh*. The *Safir*, which uses a stretched version of the *Nodong/Shahab-3* as its first stage, lifted Iran's first satellite into space in 2009. The *Simorgh* is a larger carrier rocket designed to launch heavier satellites to higher orbits. A mock-up was unveiled in 2010. The *Simorgh* was reportedly flight-tested in April 2016 and July 2017, apparently unsuccessfully on both occasions.[44] The first stage is powered by a cluster of four *Nodong* engines, while the second stage employs low-thrust steering engines adapted from the Soviet-era submarine-launched ballistic missile known as the R-27, or SS-N-6 *Serb*.

Some analysts claim that because Iran's space-launch vehicles utilise engines and other technology that was originally designed for ballistic missiles, launches of such systems are prohibited by the clause in UNSCR 2231 which refers to 'launches using such ballistic missile technology'.[45] Just because these rockets use *Nodong* engines, however, does not necessarily mean they or other technologies were originally designed for systems to deliver nuclear weapons. Engines are commonly repurposed or modified for different uses, and the intended payload depends on other parts of the missile system. The *Safir* presents a stronger case for nuclear intention, given its relation to the *Nodong*. However, a stretched version of the *Nodong* has never appeared as a ballistic missile in Iran (or, indeed, elsewhere). The case for the *Simorgh* is less clear, as it employs an engine cluster, and the steering mechanism is different from that of the *Nodong*.

Iran's satellite-launch vehicles could, in principle, be used as a springboard to developing an intermediate-range ballistic missile (IRBM), or an ICBM. However, no country has converted a satellite launcher into a liquid-fuel long-range ballistic missile, and for sound reasons. It is worth noting that in the 1970s, China did develop its *Dongfeng* (DF) long-range missiles in parallel with two versions of the *Chang Zheng* (CZ) satellite launcher that shared many components, but in both cases the versions designated for delivering nuclear payloads were subjected to full-scope flight trials as a ballistic missile, separate from the CZ satellite launches. Testing as a ballistic missile is necessary because the operational requirements, performance parameters and flight paths for satellite launchers and military missiles are very different.

India's sophisticated space programme regularly launches satellites on indigenously developed rockets which employ large, solid-fuelled boosters. India's Defence Research and Development Organization (DRDO), which is responsible for developing the nation's long-range ballistic missiles, relies on space-agency enterprises to manufacture the solid-propellant stages for these systems. While the DRDO operates independently of the space programme, it has nevertheless benefitted enormously from the experience and capabilities it has developed, although the DRDO has not explicitly transformed a satellite launcher into a ballistic missile.

There has long been concern that North Korea is developing space-launch vehicles as a cover for ballistic missiles. So far, however, the *Unha* rocket has only been used to try to orbit satellites, not to test warhead delivery. Instead, North Korea ended up designing, developing and testing three long-range missiles, the *Hwasong*-12, -14 and -15, that rely on very different technologies and hardware.

Without question, rockets designed to boost a satellite into orbit and long-range ballistic missiles employ many of the same technologies, key components and operational features. There are, however, key characteristics that differentiate satellite launchers from ballistic missiles, apart from the payload itself. Firstly, ballistic-missile payloads must survive re-entry into the earth's atmosphere. Protecting a long-range missile's payload from the extreme heat and structural loads to which it is exposed during re-entry requires the development and production of special materials, as well as testing and validation under real conditions.

Secondly, satellite-launch vehicles and long-range ballistic missiles have distinctly different trajectories to fulfil their respective missions. These different trajectories call for different propulsion systems for optimal performance. It is not possible to simply swap one engine for another and expect the missile to perform reliably. Multiple flight tests of the new configuration are needed to validate performance and reliability.

A third and less obvious difference lies in operational requirements. Before flight, satellite launchers, unlike their ballistic-missile counterparts, are prepared over a period of many days, if not weeks. Components and subsystems are checked and verified prior to launch. The mission commander has the flexibility to wait for ideal weather before initiating the countdown. If an anomaly emerges during the countdown, engineers can delay the launch, identify and fix the problem, and restart the process.

Ballistic missiles, in contrast, like other military systems, must perform reliably under a variety of operational conditions with little or no warning. These operational requirements impose a more rigorous validation scheme, which includes an extensive flight-test programme. Normally, a missile is deemed to be combat ready only after successfully completing validation testing. This latter requirement, and the need to ensure pre-launch survivability, explain why neither the US nor the Soviet Union ever converted a satellite launcher into a ballistic missile, even though the reverse process occurred frequently. China developed its early long-range missiles (DF-3, DF-4 and DF-5) and satellite launchers (CZ-1 and CZ-2) in parallel. However, running these programmes in tandem did not obviate the need to conduct over many years a full set of flight trials for the military missiles. Nor did the parallel programmes shorten the development timeline significantly.

Iran's *Safir* and *Simorgh* rockets are optimised to lift a satellite into orbit. The second stages used by both systems are powered by low-thrust, long-action-time engines, which accelerate the satellite along a path parallel to the earth's surface. A ballistic-missile trajectory must climb to higher altitudes to optimise its range capacity. An underpowered second stage would necessarily fight gravitational forces over a longer time, robbing the payload of velocity and, therefore, range.

Iran could in theory opt to modify the *Simorgh* satellite-launch platform, by replacing the second stage's propulsion system with a *Scud* or *Nodong* engine, for use as a ballistic missile, though the transformation would be neither simple nor quick. There would still be a need to flight-test the transformed *Simorgh* in a ballistic-missile role. If Iran built a ballistic missile using the *Simorgh*'s first stage, and a *Nodong* engine for the second stage, the notional missile might achieve a maximum range of 4,000–6,000 km, depending on configuration details and the payload. To reach the continental US, a powerful third stage would have to be developed for the *Simorgh*. The notional missile would remain poorly suited for use as a ballistic missile, because it would be too large and cumbersome to deploy on a mobile launcher. It would therefore have to be placed in a silo, making it an attractive target for adversaries possessing advanced reconnaissance and pre-emptive-strike capabilities.

The Soviet Union considered an analogous upgrade in 1957, when the Yangel Design Bureau suggested combining the main boosters of the R-12 and R-14 missiles to create the R-16 ICBM. The R-16 was successfully developed, but only after substantial redesign, including the development of new engines using more energetic propellants. The Soviet experience suggests that Iran would find it challenging and time-consuming to build an operational ICBM derived mainly from *Simorgh* hardware. A new missile design seems more plausible.

To ensure that Iran does not seek such modifications, it would be useful to negotiate an agreement that placed verifiable limits on the space-launch programme and applied transparency measures to confirm its purely civilian purpose. The HCoC protocols could serve as an initial foundation for promoting such transparency. Accepting the legitimacy of Iran's space-launch programme would be a hard pill to swallow for its critics. Yet such a compromise could be made without detriment to the security of Western nations, especially if part of a trade-off that restricted ballistic missiles intended for nuclear-weapons delivery.

Assessing design intent

How can one determine if Iran's missiles have been designed to carry nuclear warheads? Under the MTCR definition, all of Iran's liquid-fuel missiles (*Shahab*-1, -2 and -3, as well as the *Qiam*, *Ghadr*, *Emad* and *Khorramshahr*) would be considered 'nuclear capable'. The *Safir* and *Simorgh* satellite-launch rockets, and Iran's solid-fuel *Sajjil*-2 missile, would also fall under this definition. Iran's short-range artillery rockets, the solid-fuel *Fateh*-110 and its derivatives, the *Khalij Fars* and *Hormuz* missiles, do not, however, exceed the MTCR threshold. It is unclear if the *Fateh*-313 can carry 500 kg loads beyond 300 km, though a preliminary assessment of the missile's performance indicates it falls short of the MTCR limits.

In addition to falling below the MTCR threshold for performance, the *Fateh*-110's development history, its use in war games and deployment with the regular army's conventional-artillery units – instead of the IRGC Aerospace Forces responsible for strategic missiles – offers a compelling argument that the rocket was not designed and developed to carry a nuclear payload. Iran's transfer of the *Fateh*-110 to Hizbullah is consistent with this argument.

On the same basis, the *Khalij Fars* and *Hormuz* missiles, as well as the *Fateh*-313, can be judged non-nuclear, as can the *Zulfiqar*. None of these *Fateh*-110 derivatives exceed the MTCR threshold, and all were developed to conduct battlefield missions aimed at denying an aggressor its military aims.

Scud export model for conventional warheads

Iran's *Shahab*-1 and -2 are clones of the Soviet *Scud*-B and *Scud*-C missiles, respectively. The *Scud*-B (R-17/8K14) was designed and developed to replace the *Scud*-A (R-11M/8K11). The 170 km range R-11M was armed with the 3N10 nuclear warhead (containing the RDS-4 nuclear charge), and deployed with the Reserve of the Supreme High Command (RVGK), which was responsible for the Soviet Union's nuclear weapons. In December 1959, then Soviet premier Nikita Khrushchev converted the RVGK missile brigades into the new Strategic Rocket Force (RVSN). The R-11M units were not included in the RVSN; instead, these were reclassified as Operational–Tactical Missile Brigades, which were placed under the control of the Soviet ground forces and assigned to armies. The Soviet ground force's artillery branch was renamed the 'missile and artillery forces' as a consequence of the changes.

Soviet missile concern SKB-385, headed by V.P. Makeyev, began developing the *Scud*-B in April 1958. Initial flight tests were conducted in December 1959, and the missile was first deployed to the military in 1964. The *Scud*-B was designed primarily as a nuclear-delivery system, though a family of standardised, 1,000 kg warheads was developed. The first warhead assigned to the *Scud*-B was the 8F14 design, which contained a charge with a 10 kilotonne capacity. A few years after the missile was deployed, the 9N33 warhead, which has a 300 kt yield, replaced the 8F14. When armed with either warhead, the *Scud*-B missile measures 11.2 m in length, and has a diameter of 0.9 m.

The conventional 8F44 warhead was developed for export versions of the *Scud*-B. Designated R-17E/8K14E, the conventionally armed missiles were exported to Soviet allies, typically as part of an arms package designed to equip an army division. When armed with a conventional warhead, the exported *Scud*-B at 10.9 m is slightly shorter than the nuclear version.

The *Scud*-C (R-17M/9M77) is an extended-range version of the *Scud*-B. Development began in March 1963, with flight trials at Kapustin Yar commencing in 1964 and ending in 1967. The *Scud*-C never entered service with the Soviet military, though the missile may have been exported to North Korea in the late 1980s.

The *Scud*-C has the same external dimensions as the conventional version of the *Scud*-B, but carries about 580 kg of additional liquid propellant and a smaller warhead (about 750 kg). A common bulkhead separates the fuel and oxidiser tanks in the *Scud*-C, a configuration that allows the missile to hold the additional fuel. Combined, the added propellant, lighter warhead and a few additional modifications extend the *Scud*-Cs range to about 500 km. There is no publicly available evidence to indicate that a nuclear warhead was ever designed for use on the *Scud*-C.

Although the *Scud*-B was originally designed to be nuclear-armed, the Soviet Union developed and fielded conventional versions of the missile. Only the conventional version of the *Scud*-B (R-17E) was exported to non-Warsaw Pact countries, including Egypt, Libya and North Korea. The *Scud*-C was never fielded as a nuclear-armed missile. It is reasonable to conclude, therefore, that the exported *Scud*-B and the *Scud*-C were designed to carry conventional warheads.

Iran's *Shahab*-1 and *Shahab*-2 missiles are 10.944 m in length, matching precisely the external dimensions of the conventionally armed *Scud*-B (R-17E) and *Scud*-C (R-17M) missiles. Photographs, videos and performance data for the *Shahab*-1 and the R-17E are indistinguishable, indicating that the Iranian and Soviet missiles share a design heritage. Similarly, the *Shahab*-2 appears to be a clone of the R-17M.

The *Shahab*-1 and -2 missiles exceed the MTCR threshold, suggesting that they are capable of carrying nuclear warheads.

However, the text of UNSCR 2231 proscribes missiles 'designed to be capable' of carrying a nuclear weapon – not missiles that are capable of being fitted with a nuclear warhead. The design heritages of the *Shahab*-1 and *Shahab*-2 – the exported *Scud*-B and the *Scud*-C, respectively – indicate that both missiles were designed to carry conventional, not nuclear, payloads.

During his unveiling of the atomic archives smuggled out of Iran, Netanyahu presented a slide labelled, 'Integrating nuclear warheads on Missiles'. The slide's subtitle indicates that the two design drawings shown on the slide related to Iran's *Shahab*-3. However, closer examination of the two drawings creates some confusion. The illustration on the right-hand side of the slide is clearly related to the *Shahab*-3. The schematic on the left is presumed to be related to the *Shahab*-3 but armed with a larger-diameter bomb design. It is possible, however, that the drawing on the left could instead depict a *Scud*-B/*Shahab*-1 nosecone equipped with an implosion device with a diameter of about 585 mm, which is the same as the bomb design shown on the right-side illustration of the *Shahab*-3 warhead. The warhead design on the left does not fully contain the bomb design. If the base section of the warhead were extended by 20–25 centimetres, the bomb would be fully housed. This modification would necessarily add 20–25 cm to the total length of the missile, making it consistent with the length of the Soviet Union's nuclear design of the *Scud*-C (R-17). A *Shahab*-1 or -2 with a length of 11.0 m or more would indicate that it is designed to carry a modified warhead, presumably a nuclear one. *Shahab*-1 and -2 missiles measuring 10.944 m would still be understood to carry conventional payloads.

In 2010, Iran introduced the liquid-fuel *Qiam* missile, which is designed to carry a 500 kg warhead to more than 700 km. It is armed with a conventional warhead, and according to Iranian media was among the half-dozen missiles fired at ISIS positions in Syria in June 2017.[46] The *Qiam* was most likely intended to counter missile defences by incorporating a separating warhead into the design. A separating warhead is more difficult for radars to detect and track than a warhead attached to the missile's fuselage. Although based on the *Scud*-C, the modifications were so extensive that only the *Qiam*'s engine is the same. So although the *Scud*-C that Iran imported was originally designed to carry a conventional payload, this lineage does not necessarily carry over to the *Qiam*. It must be noted that the *Qiam*'s nosecone is the same as that of the *Ghadr*, minus the flange that attaches the re-entry vehicle to the *Ghadr*'s 1.25 m diameter. The weapons compartment of the *Ghadr*, and thus the *Qiam*, is too small to fit the Iranian bomb design detailed in intelligence released by Israel. Given Iran's economy in employing the same warhead for different systems, this nosecone presumably makes the *Qiam* a system designed to carry conventional warheads, and not nuclear ones.

Shahab-3 nuclear-delivery origin

The design history of the North Korean *Nodong* missile, and thus Iran's *Shahab*-3, is unclear. Some analysts contend that North Korea designed and developed the *Nodong* by 'scaling up' the *Scud*-B missile that it had previously reverse-engineered from a handful of sample exported *Scud*-Bs (R-17E) received from Egypt. Although the *Nodong*'s engine generates twice as much thrust as the *Scud*-B's 9D21 engine, the two systems share many common design features. Though the *Nodong*'s external dimensions are larger than those of the *Scud*-B by a factor of $\sqrt{2}$, the two systems look very similar. The *Scud*-B and *Nodong* employ the same propellant combination.

Others argue that the *Nodong* was originally designed and produced in small numbers by the Soviet Union, and transferred to North Korea in the late 1980s. A handful of academics and missile specialists from Russia have stated explicitly that the *Nodong*'s engine is a product of the Isayev Design Bureau, the developer responsible for the *Scud*-B's 9D21 engine.[47] It is also noteworthy that the *Nodong*'s dimensions are consistent with a 'scaled-up' version of the nuclear-armed *Scud*-B (R-17), not the conventionally armed export model (R-17E). North Korea did not possess a nuclear version of the *Scud*-B. However, there is no record of the Soviet Union flight-testing or deploying a missile like the *Nodong*.

In either case, it is likely that the missile was designed to carry nuclear weapons. The Soviet Union was known to be developing a range of ballistic missiles for its burgeoning nuclear-weapons programme in the 1950s and 1960s. The sophistication of the production methods used to build the *Nodong* missiles seen in Iran, North Korea and Pakistan are consistent with other missiles designed and manufactured by the Soviets in the 1960s. Therefore, if the *Nodong* was developed in the Soviet Union, it was undoubtedly designed for nuclear weapons, as were the other missiles developed during this era.

If North Korea designed and developed the *Nodong*, it is reasonable to assume it was designated for nuclear-weapons delivery. Pyongyang was actively pursuing a nuclear-weapons capability around the time the *Nodong* was developed. The *Scud*-B, which North Korea already possessed, had several shortcomings as Pyongyang's primary nuclear-delivery platform. Its range was limited to 300 km, leaving it incapable of targeting all of the Korean Peninsula. The range of both the *Scud*-B and the *Scud*-C fell well short of Japan. It would make little sense for Pyongyang to possess nuclear weapons that it could not deliver to key targets. The *Nodong*'s reach is large enough to cover all of South Korea, and most of Japan. Moreover, North Korea was in the early stages of nuclear-weapons development. Its scientists may have been uncertain about the size and mass of a first-generation nuclear warhead. The *Nodong*'s larger size and greater lifting capacity offered North Korea's engineers greater flexibility and posed less risk should any nuclear device end up being bigger or heavier than anticipated. While the contemporaneous development of nuclear weapons and the *Nodong* does not prove the missile was designed for nuclear use, there is every reason to believe North Korea understood that the *Nodong* would be capable of delivering its first-generation nuclear weapon.

There is little doubt that the *Nodong* was originally designed for nuclear-weapons delivery, which may explain why Iran originally imported the missile from North Korea. Tehran perceives Israel as posing an existential threat which needs to be deterred, and the *Shahab*-3's payload and range capabilities mean Iran can target Israel with either conventional warheads, or a notional nuclear warhead. Documentation contained in the aforementioned laptop smuggled out of Iran in 2004, and the atomic archives released by Israel in 2018, indicate that Tehran at the very least explored nuclear designs for the *Shahab*-3 missile. Yet Tehran's programme to extend the range of the *Shahab*-3 through a series of modifications – resulting in the *Ghadr*, which has a nosecone too small for a first-generation nuclear weapon, and which could reach Israel when launched from positions hundreds of kilometres from Iran's border with Iraq – is consistent with a defence and deterrence strategy that relies on conventionally armed missiles.

In 2015, Iran unveiled and flight-tested the *Emad* missile – a variant of the *Ghadr* – equipped with a warhead that can apparently be steered to its targets during re-entry into the atmosphere. Iran argues that the *Emad* is designed for the accurate delivery of conventional warheads. This may indeed have been the basis for the *Emad*'s development, though as highlighted above, Cold War history shows that precision-guided missiles armed with nuclear warheads can be used for counter-force missions aimed at destroying hardened targets.

Iran's *Sajjil-2* is a two-stage, solid-fuel ballistic missile capable of carrying a 700 kg warhead to about 2,000 km. Iran is the only country to develop a ballistic missile with a range of 2,000 km without first possessing nuclear weapons. *Sajjil* missiles flight-tested from 2008–11 were equipped with a *Ghadr* nosecone, which, as noted above, was redesigned to be too small to accommodate a first-generation nuclear-implosion device. The *Sajjil*'s maximum range is roughly 400 km greater than that of the *Ghadr*. The additional range does not enable Iran to strike any new, strategically important targets. It does, however, facilitate the launch of a heavier warhead from positions deep inside Iran, making the missile less vulnerable to pre-emptive attack. The *Ghadr*, if fitted with a payload of one tonne, would see its maximum range reduced to just over 1,100 km, meaning that to strike Israel, it would have to be launched from a site near Iran's border with Iraq. The *Sajjil* could still be launched a considerable distance east of the border when carrying a heavier payload. It is reasonable to conclude that the *Sajjil* was designed as a more flexible and capable backup for the *Ghadr* missile.

Khorramshahr

It is difficult to make firm judgements about the technical basis, origins, performance capacity and intended purpose of the *Khorramshahr* missile. It is almost certainly large and powerful enough to deliver a first-generation nuclear warhead well beyond the MTCR parameters. The available evidence – size, photographs, a launch video from a test in September 2017 and statements by Tehran – indicates that at a minimum, the missile can reach 2,000 km when carrying a 1,000 kg payload. With a 500 kg payload, it might be able to fly as far as 2,800 km, although this is a very rough estimate. Iran could therefore easily exceed its self-declared limit of 2,000 km. Adopting a verifiable 2,000 km limit would likely mean abandoning the *Khorramshahr*.

The *Khorramshahr's* design appears to be similar to that of the North Korean *Musudan* (*Hwasong*-10), itself presumably designed for nuclear delivery. Pyongyang began testing the *Musudan* in April 2016, which coincided with North Korea's accelerated nuclear testing. *Musudan* tests were followed by those of the longer-range *Hwasong*-12, -14 and -15 missiles, which Pyongyang contends are designed for nuclear delivery. The *Musudan* is derived from the Soviet-era R-27 (SS-N-6) submarine-launched ballistic missile – which was designed for nuclear use – and uses much of the R-27's critical hardware. The *Khorramshahr's* lineage certainly implies that it too is designed to be at least capable of carrying a nuclear weapon.

Iran's *Khorramshahr* has a much larger nosecone than those seen on North Korea's *Musudan*, or formerly deployed on the Soviet R-27. The missile's estimated performance indicates that it can carry a heavy payload – perhaps one weighing 1,800 kg, as claimed by Iran.[48] The lethal radius of a conventional warhead weighing 1,800 kg is only 20% greater than that of one weighing 1,000 kg, so arming a missile with the larger warhead would only marginally improve its military utility. Alternatively, the greater volume of the nosecone could accommodate a nuclear weapon with a diameter of just over one metre. This is not proof, however, that *Khorramshahr* is designed to carry such a nuclear weapon.

It is possible that the nosecone might be a shroud that is discarded after the *Khorramshahr's* engines cut off. Under the shroud, the missile may have a re-entry vehicle or a warhead that is similar to, or the same as, that of the *Musudan* or the R-27. This seems unlikely, however, because it is not strictly necessary, and it would reduce the missile's reach by 300–400 km. More probably, if the missile is equipped with a shroud, it is to protect (or hide) one or more conventional warheads. Iran has suggested the missile can carry multiple warheads, each of which would very likely be too small to be nuclear.[49] A multiple-warhead design is sensible if Iran is trying to counter missile defences by saturating their radars with many targets. Given the *Khorramshahr*'s design heritage and its capabilities, it is reasonable, though not conclusive, to suggest that the missile is designed to be nuclear-capable.

Conclusions

Iran's ballistic missiles have sparked concerns that they could be potential delivery platforms for a future nuclear weapon. Although missile tests do not violate the JCPOA or any other international treaty, Western powers frequently assert that UNSCR 2231 proscribes Iran's testing of missiles that the MTCR threshold deems inherently capable of delivering nuclear weapons. However, UNSCR 2231 does not explicitly refer to the MTCR, or its performance threshold, which eight of Iran's 13 current ballistic-missile systems exceed. Rather, it calls upon Iran 'not to undertake any activity related to ballistic missiles designed to be capable of delivering nuclear weapons'. The language of UNSCR 2231 introduces an element of intent that is lacking in the MTCR and in previous Security Council resolutions concerning Iranian missiles.

For Iran's medium-range *Shahab-3* system, there is strong evidence of nuclear intent. Schematics turned over by a defector in 2004, and documents made public by Israel in May 2018, provide evidence of Iranian efforts to fit a nuclear-implosion weapon into the *Shahab-3*'s re-entry vehicle. Clearly, any Iranian missile equipped with the *Shahab-3* re-entry vehicle can be said to be designed to be nuclear-capable – a conclusion further supported by its direct linkage to North Korea's *Nodong* missile, which was developed to deliver nuclear weapons.

In 2004, Iran introduced a new re-entry vehicle design for the *Shahab*-3, which is too small to house the nuclear-implosion device outlined in the Iranian documents. The *Ghadr*, as the new missile was called, along with the *Sajjil*-2 and *Qiam*, which are equipped with the same nosecone, can therefore be said to have been designed for non-nuclear use. This assessment would have to change if Iran developed a miniaturised nuclear warhead.

Iran's *Emad* missile is a variant of the *Ghadr*, indicating that by lineage it is designed for non-nuclear use. Its re-entry vehicle is, in principle, large enough to house the nuclear weapon described in Iranian documents. However, it is unclear if the re-entry vehicle would be aerodynamically stable during re-entry without placing significant ballast near the tip of the nosecone. A final judgement of the *Emad*'s design intent requires more information about the flight worthiness of the re-entry vehicle.

The design intent of Iran's *Khorramshahr* missile is harder to judge because of the dearth of reliable information about its design and capabilities. It appears to be derived from North Korea's *Musudan* (*Hwasong*-10) missile, which employs technology and hardware from the Soviet Union's submarine-launched R-27 (SS-N-6) ballistic missile. The *Musudan* and R-27 were designed to carry a nuclear weapon. The *Khorramshahr*, if it is indeed linked to these North Korean and Soviet nuclear-armed missiles, can be judged to have been designed for nuclear-weapons delivery.

Iran's *Shahab*-1 and *Shahab*-2 are based on export models of the Soviet *Scud*-B and *Scud*-C missiles that were designed to carry conventional weapons. While these missiles exceed the MTCR threshold, it would be incorrect to assert that they were designed for nuclear weapons. Furthermore, Iran initially acquired the conventionally armed *Shahab-1* in the mid-1980s for use against Iraq during the war. This judgement applies only to Shahab-1 and -2 missiles that measure 10.944 m in length. Longer versions of either of these missiles would need reassessment to ensure that they are not designed to be nuclear-capable.

The *Fateh-110* family of missiles, which includes the *Khalij Fars*, *Hormuz*, *Fateh-313* and *Zulfiqar*, carries conventional warheads, and these systems were developed for use on the battlefield. Further, their nosecones are too narrow to house the nuclear-warhead design featured in Iranian documents.

Iran has also developed two space-launch vehicles, the *Safir* and *Simorgh*. Both are optimised and configured for launching satellites. Neither has been tested as a ballistic missile. Indeed, they would require significant modifications to perform in that role. It is therefore difficult to argue that the *Safir* and *Simorgh* are designed for nuclear-weapons delivery. It should be noted that no country has repurposed a liquid-fuelled satellite-launch vehicle into a long-range ballistic missile.

Given the central role that conventionally armed ballistic missiles play in Iran's defence and deterrence posture, it is implausible that Iran would agree to surrender them voluntarily. Iran has signalled a possible willingness to limit the range of its missiles to 2,000 km. If agreement on such a ceiling was reached, Iran's missiles would only threaten targets within the Middle East. Verifying that Iran does not have an ICBM programme would neuter the most alarmist condemnations of its missile programme. It may be necessary, however, to accept a restricted and transparent space-launch capability. Meanwhile, Iran's neighbours will have to live with its conventionally armed missiles, for which missile-defence systems would be an effective countermeasure. If negotiations were to take place over Iran's short- and medium-range missiles, the US and its allies should give priority to removing the systems most clearly designed to deliver nuclear weapons: the *Shahab-3*, the *Khorramshahr* and, potentially, the *Emad*.

for uranium enrichment. US President Barack Obama realised that the best way to turn this around was to accept Iran's de facto right to enrichment. This compromise played a larger role than coercion through sanctions in inducing Iran to make its own compromises. Although intrusive verification measures would last forever, Iran simply would not accept unbounded limits on production. As in most arms-control agreements, 'sunset' provisions were negotiated. Meanwhile, in the West it was expected that the limits might need to be extended at the end of the period, if doubts still remained about Iran's nuclear intentions.

The early decision to limit the scope of negotiations to the nuclear issue was also key to their success. Concerns about Iran's regional activities and internal repression, while important, are of secondary strategic importance: only with nuclear weapons would Iran present a direct national-security threat to states beyond its neighbourhood. Trying to include regional issues would have further complicated a task that was already complex. Later claims that sanctions relief enabled Iran to expand its influence in the region are unfounded. Most of the money that Iran obtained through sanctions relief was used for economic development and infrastructure, and Iran's support for militant groups over the years has been relatively cheap and low-tech, and is not correlated with the size of the state budget.

One of the last compromises struck before concluding the deal was the decision not to require Iran to acknowledge its past nuclear-weapons development work. Iran was to address questions about the matter, but whether its answers were satisfactory was left to the discretion of the International Atomic Energy Agency (IAEA). Iran was opaque and reticent in its replies and constricted inspector access to the Parchin military base where nuclear development work had taken place. Nevertheless, the IAEA was able to conclude in November

2015 that, contrary to Iran's claims, it had in fact engaged in coordinated research on nuclear weapons. Given that this research took place in the past and was judged not to have advanced beyond an exploratory stage, the parties agreed not to let a lack of admission or full accounting delay implementation of the JCPOA in January 2016. This judgement made sense, but it planted the seeds for much of the condemnation that was to follow.

Mutual compromise is the essence of negotiation. Iran made as many concessions as it was granted, and rolled back its nuclear programme before it received any sanctions relief. Iran had to send 98% of its low-enriched-uranium (LEU) stockpile out of the country, put over two-thirds of its centrifuges out of commission and prevent plutonium production by filling up the core of its Arak research reactor with concrete. These concessions by Iran were far more meaningful than Obama's heavily criticised move to release to Iran just over US$50 billion of its own revenue from oil sales that had previously been frozen under sanctions.

Most of the criticism heaped on the deal by Obama's political opponents was based on the notion that a better deal could have been negotiated, had he been less eager to achieve diplomatic success. Counterfactuals by nature cannot be disproven, but the claim that Iran could have been forced to make unilateral concessions of the kind demanded by critics is naïve and unrealistic. As secretary of state, John Kerry rightly derided opponents' demands for full enrichment cessation forever as the 'unicorn' deal. The sunset provisions cannot be undone without undoing the deal altogether.

Criticism by JCPOA opponents of its verification arrangements is unbalanced, but stems partly from the false expectations raised by the Obama administration when officials said that inspections under the deal would be allowed 'anytime, anywhere'. Such a verification condition can be imposed after defeating a nation in war, as in the case of Iraq after the First Gulf War (1990–91), but no undefeated sovereign state would allow unfettered access to its military bases. Instead, the JCPOA provided for IAEA inspections when needed, where needed. This right was clarified through an expedited inspection-request process for 'complementary access' to sites where the IAEA had legitimate questions about possible nuclear activity or anomalies in Iran's reporting. Under the JCPOA, Iran accepted the most robust nuclear-verification system anywhere in the world.

IAEA Director General Yukiya Amano insists that the agency has access to any location in Iran which it needs to see, and that its right to access is not limited to civilian sites. Critics dispute this, citing claims by Iranian officials that military bases are off limits to the IAEA. Such claims, made for domestic consumption and to protect military secrets, are belied by the fact that inspectors have visited Iranian military facilities more than 20 times in the past. The IAEA insists that Iran has not denied any inspection-access requests under the JCPOA. If inspectors have not asked to go to any military sites since the deal came into effect, it is because no reporting anomalies that require such visits have arisen. Upholding its independence and neutrality, the agency would never agree to ask for a base inspection for the purpose of trapping Iran into saying no, as suggested by some JCPOA critics.

Verification typically starts with non-intrusive measures, such as scientific papers, import/export data, overhead imagery and media reporting, as well as intelligence briefings by member states. If questions stemming from analysis of such sources arise, the agency seeks additional information from Iran and, if this is unsatisfactory, requests an inspection. (For declared sites, inspections take place frequently.)

The IAEA's decision in 2015 not to require full clarification of Iran's past nuclear-weapons research exposed a key vulnerability of the JCPOA. Iran's refusal to admit to this work and its careful storage of files detailing that research – tens of thousands of which were stolen from Tehran by Israeli intelligence early in 2018 – indicates that it has not ruled out resuming weapons development in the future. It has been clear for some time, of course, that Iran has a barely recessed nuclear hedging strategy. This is no reason to object to the JCPOA, however. To the contrary: it is precisely because Iran's nuclear intentions cannot be trusted that the limits and intrusive verification requirements of the JCPOA are vitally important. Without them, regional security and global non-proliferation are imperilled.

Short of trying to compel Iran to renegotiate the JCPOA to accept compromises that it refused to accommodate before, there are several ways in which the accord could be improved upon by using established mechanisms. The Joint Commission (the body comprised of the JCPOA parties, which oversees the implementation of the accord) has a proven track record in clarifying technical ambiguities that were left undefined in the deal, such as the number of advanced centrifuges that can be operated for research and development, and IAEA monitoring of such operations. The Joint Commission should clarify the role of the IAEA in verifying the unprecedented restrictions that Section T imposed on certain activities that would contribute to nuclear-weapons development. This will require cooperative diplomacy with Russia to persuade it to drop its veto of such verification. Iran's production of more heavy water than it needs for domestic purposes should also be addressed, as critics have magnified the two overages of Iran's heavy-water stockpiles. Limits on heavy water should be tightened, so that they apply to excess product sent to Oman or elsewhere for storage prior to sale.

Most importantly, the thorny issue of inspections at military bases needs to be addressed, so that a prolonged absence of IAEA access to bases does not set a negative norm whereby Iran's military facilities are implicitly accepted as being off-limits for the IAEA. Rather than making politically charged demands that Iran will inevitably resist, however, the IAEA should seek visits to selective military facilities in the context of working to reach the broader conclusion. To draw this conclusion, the IAEA will need to put firmly to rest all lingering concerns about Parchin and any other military sites where nuclear activity is suspected of having occurred in the past. The IAEA must seek access to sites where the 'atomic archive' documents seized by Israel indicate that nuclear-weapons development work was taking place or where equipment and documents were stored. While not a requirement of the JCPOA, the IAEA may also need to check the status of dual-use equipment that Iran imported in the past and which may now be located at military sites to draw the broader conclusion. Because Iran wants the legitimacy that the broader conclusion would entail, it has a reason to cooperate with the IAEA in allowing certain military-site visits.

The remaining parties to the JCPOA should also endeavour to keep in place the Procurement Channel that was established to monitor Iran's acquisition of nuclear-related material for the limited programme allowed by the accord. The idea was that having such a legal mechanism would curb illicit procurement – one of the major concerns surrounding Iran's nuclear programme. The purpose of the Procurement Channel is to review proposals by states seeking to engage in trade with Iran involving nuclear and non-nuclear civilian end uses. Prior to the JCPOA, such trade was prohibited by UN Security Council resolutions. The JCPOA changed this approach, allowing transfers of nuclear or dual-use goods, technology and related services, provided that the Security Council gives its approval on a case-by-case basis.

With certain exceptions, a foreign company that wishes to sell Iran goods that may be nuclear-related which are approved by the established licensing process in its home country must apply through the Procurement Working Group, the composition of which mirrors that of the Joint Commission. If the items are intended for a nuclear application, the IAEA must also approve. Under a rigorous verification process, the exporting state assumes responsibility for conducting end-use checks, but the Iranian government assumes ultimate responsibility for ensuring that no goods purchased via the channel are diverted to illicit use.

Despite a relatively low level of activity, the mechanism has been working, with 37 proposals submitted as of June 2018, 34 of which have been processed. A total of 24 were approved, three disapproved and seven withdrawn. Interestingly, 13 of these proposals were submitted in the first half of 2018, seemingly defying uncertainty about the JCPOA's future engendered by the hostility of the Trump administration.

Allegations of dual-use goods transferred to Iran outside the Procurement Channel outlined in the June 2018 report by the UN secretary-general raise some concerns, not least with respect to the effectiveness of the dispute-resolution processes available. A proper investigative mechanism is needed, and the UN Secretariat should be empowered to play this role. Before the JCPOA came into effect in 2016, an independent UN Panel of Experts had been tasked with monitoring the implementation of UN sanctions on Iran and investigating any possible violations. The Secretariat's mandate is much weaker in this regard. With allegations of non-compliance on the agenda, this deficiency should be addressed in order to preserve the credibility of the mechanism.

At the beginning of negotiations, Western parties sought to include Iran's ballistic missiles, given their intrinsic connection to nuclear weapons. In the face of Chinese, Iranian and Russian objections, the West gave in, justifying the compromise on the basis that without nuclear warheads the missiles posed far less of a threat. Yet when the JCPOA limits expire and Iran is free to enrich as much uranium as it wants as quickly as it can, having capable ballistic missiles as a delivery system would be crucial to any future nuclear-weapons strategy.

JCPOA critics are wrong to claim that Iran's ballistic missiles have little purpose other than to be mated with future nuclear weapons. Iran acquired its first ballistic missiles in the mid-1980s to counter Iraq's air and missile strikes against its cities and economic infrastructure. The apparent success of its retaliatory strikes convinced Iran of the value of missiles. Considering missiles to be essential to both deterrence and defence, Tehran steadily thereafter expanded its missile arsenal.

It is certainly not the case that every Iranian ballistic-missile system is explicitly linked to nuclear-weapons development. Iran's shorter-range *Fateh*-110 family of missiles is probably not capable of carrying first-generation nuclear weapons, and was almost certainly not designed for that purpose. Iran's use of *Zulfiqar* missiles against a position of the Islamic State, also known as ISIS or ISIL, in Syria in June 2017, too, was a clear demonstration of a non-nuclear aim.

On the other hand, Iran's claim that its missiles are only conventional is disingenuous. It possesses 13 different types of ballistic missile, giving it the largest and most diverse missile force in the region – although not the most lethal or longest range (distinctions held by Israel and possibly Saudi Arabia). Of these 13 systems, eight have ranges over 300 km if fitted with a payload exceeding 500 kg. Under guidelines established by the Missile Technology Control Regime (MTCR), an informal export-control arrangement among 35 countries, 300 km/500 kg is the threshold for presumptive export denial. Missiles exceeding this threshold are generally judged to be inherently capable of delivering nuclear weapons.

Whether Iran intends for its missile systems over this threshold to carry nuclear weapons is another question. The issue of intent was introduced by United Nations Security Council Resolution 2231, adopted in July 2015 to endorse the JCPOA and supersede previous resolutions on Iran. Under the new measure, Iran is 'called upon not to undertake any activity related to ballistic missiles designed to be capable of delivering nuclear weapons' for eight years. In addition to the hortatory verb 'calls upon' (replacing the former mandatory ban on missile development), UNSCR 2231 inserted 'designed to' in order to address the intended purpose of the missiles in question, although the term was not defined.

The MTCR guidelines are not the only criteria by which to judge whether Iran's missiles are designed to be nuclear-capable. Another way to assess whether missiles are designed to be nuclear-capable is to trace their lineage. Iran's *Shahab*-1 and *Shahab*-2 systems, with 300 km and 500 km ranges respectively, are based on export versions of Soviet *Scuds* that were designed to carry conventional weapons. Iran's medium-range systems have a different lineage.

Intelligence information can also guide analysis of Iran's missiles. Nuclear-weapons designs smuggled out of Iran demonstrate efforts to fit a nuclear-implosion weapon into the re-entry vehicle of the *Shahab*-3. This system was therefore clearly designed to be nuclear-capable. Its descent from North Korea's *Nodong* missile is another clear indication of this intent. Similarly, the *Khorramshahr* has strong connections to nuclear-armed missiles – the Soviet R-27 and the North Korean *Musudan*

– although there is some ambiguity about Iran's intentions for further development of this system.

The *Ghadr*, *Sajjil* and *Qiam* are often said to be nuclear-capable, but the weapons bay in these three systems is too small to accommodate the nuclear weapon in the Iranian blueprint that Israeli Prime Minister Benjamin Netanyahu displayed in May 2018. Iran would need a smaller weapon for these systems to be nuclear-delivery vehicles. The case for the *Emad* is more complicated; while the presumptive bomb may fit its nosecone, it is unclear whether the re-entry vehicle would be stable during return through the atmosphere. Iran's claim that an emphasis on accuracy for the *Emad* belies any nuclear purpose is not convincing, however, given that accuracy remains an important factor when attacking hardened targets with nuclear weapons.

Iran's carrier rockets, the *Safir* and *Simorgh*, are designed and optimised to lift satellites into low-earth orbit. The second-stage propulsion systems of both rockets rely on low-thrust, long-action-time engines, which is ideal for accelerating a satellite on a path parallel to the earth's surface and into a sustainable orbit, but poorly suited for ballistic-missile trajectories, which reach higher altitudes. This is one reason no country has converted a satellite launcher into a long-range liquid-fuel ballistic missile. There are others, including the very different operational needs of such systems and the requirement that a missile's payload survive the stresses experienced during atmospheric re-entry. A strong case can be made that the *Safir* and *Simorgh* were designed specifically for space launches, not nuclear-weapons delivery.

Demands that the deal be renegotiated to ban Iran's ballistic missiles are wholly unrealistic. Ballistic missiles are central to Iran's deterrence posture and will remain so for the foreseeable future. The priority assigned to ballistic missiles is reflected by the size and scope of Iran's arsenal, the largest and most diverse in the region. Given their centrality to the nation's defences, Iran cannot be expected to surrender its missiles voluntarily. Even if Iran acquires advanced military aircraft when UN-imposed limits on arms sales are lifted or expire in the coming years, ballistic missiles will continue to play a prominent role in its force structure. Recognising this, the United States and its allies should not seek the impossible goal of eliminating all of Iran's missiles. Rather, concerned states should focus on constraining the medium-range systems that were clearly designed to deliver nuclear weapons. They will have to learn to live with Iran's shorter-range systems that were not designed for nuclear weapons, though negotiations should seek constraints on their capabilities.

The accord was running smoothly up until 8 May 2018, when President Donald Trump announced that he would withdraw the US. Apart from two instances in 2016 when the vaguely worded limits on heavy-water storage were briefly exceeded by miniscule amounts, Iran has faithfully honoured its commitments under the JCPOA. Politicised claims about Iranian violations are demonstrably incorrect. Iran often pressed the envelope on research and development limits that were not clearly spelled out, but Iran's activities in this regard presented no proliferation risk and constituted no breach of the accord. The false claims contributed to the political narrative propagated by Trump, that the JCPOA was a 'terrible deal'.

The withdrawal of the US from the JCPOA was reckless. The issues Trump touted as reasons for withdrawal could have been addressed while maintaining US commitments. There was no need to walk away from the deal without an alternative in place. Alarming every partner, save four neighbours that are implacable enemies of Iran, the action isolated Washington and undermined its credibility around the world, while needlessly increasing the risk of nuclear proliferation and further conflict in the Middle East.

Whether the JCPOA can survive depends largely on Iran. On 23 May 2018, Iran's Supreme Leader Sayyid Ali Khamenei set out six conditions that Europe would have to meet if it wanted Iran to continue to uphold the accord, including pledges that Iran's oil sales would not be impeded and that European banks would guarantee financial transactions with Iran. If these trade-related conditions were not difficult enough, he added two other conditions that France, Germany and the United Kingdom would have difficulty swallowing: that they promise not to ask Iran about its ballistic-missile programme or its regional activities.[1]

In the months that followed, however, Iran seems to have adjusted its sights, realising that staying in the JCPOA, even without Europe meeting Khamenei's demands, is to its advantage. A telling moment came when Trump chose to lead a debate on Iran in the Security Council on 26 September 2018 and found himself alone.[2] This reinforced a view in Iran that there are political and diplomatic benefits in being seen by the rest of the world as the compliant party, with Washington isolated. These and the remaining economic benefits of observing the deal would be sacrificed if Iran broke out of the limits. Moreover, Tehran would derive no security advantage by doing so. Israel and/or the US would likely undertake airstrikes to stop any Iranian move towards a nuclear-weapon capability. Leaving the JCPOA, or, indeed, the Non-Proliferation Treaty (NPT) itself, as some Iranian hardliners urge, would be seen as signalling weapons intentions and thus trigger consideration of military action.

It is uncertain, however, how long the Iranian government can remain patient in adhering to the JCPOA. President Hassan Rouhani faces domestic pressure from the increasing ranks of hardliners who insist that as a matter of national pride, Iran cannot continue to be taken advantage of by unilaterally adhering to an agreement the US has broken. 'Respect' in being treated equally and fairly matters to Iran.[3] On the one hand, actions by European and other partners in keeping open banking channels will help keep Iran in the deal because it shows respect for Iran's adherence, even if it does not produce much in the way of tangible benefits. On the other side, disrespect by the US in the form of unrelenting sanctions and rhetoric serves to antagonise Iran. In the aftermath of Trump's decision, the JCPOA – which made the region and the world more stable – is on life support just three and a half years after it was signed. Its demise would be regrettable.

NOTES

Introduction

1 'Iran's Statement at IAEA Emergency Meeting', Mehr News Agency, 10 August 2005.

2 David M. Halbfinger, David E. Sanger and Ronen Bergman, 'Israel Says Secret Files Detail Iran's Nuclear Subterfuge', *New York Times,* 30 April 2018, https://www.nytimes.com/2018/04/30/world/middleeast/israel-iran-nuclear-netanyahu.html.

3 See IISS, *Nuclear Black Markets: Pakistan, A.Q. Khan and the rise of proliferation networks – A net assessment* (London: IISS, 2007).

4 Paulina Izewicz, 'Assessing the JCPOA Procurement Channel', IISS, 29 March 2018, https://www.iiss.org/blogs/analysis/2018/03/jcpoa-procurement-channel.

5 Michael Elleman and Mark Fitzpatrick, 'Are Iran's ballistic missiles designed to be nuclear capable?', IISS, 28 February 2018, https://www.iiss.org/blogs/analysis/2018/02/iran-missiles-nuclear-capable.

Chapter One

1 This chapter draws on the following pieces previously published by the author: 'Relief', *Survival: Global Politics and Strategy*, vol. 57, no. 3, June–July 2015, pp. 219–26; 'The good, the bad and the ugly in the Iran nuclear deal', *Prospect*, 14 July 2015, http://www.prospectmagazine.co.uk/world/the-good-the-bad-and-the-ugly-in-the-iran-nuclear-deal; 'Iran: A good deal', *Survival: Global Politics and Strategy*, vol. 57, no. 5, October–November 2015, pp. 47–52; 'Three strikes against claims that Iran is violating the nuclear accord', IISS, 27 July 2017, https://www.iiss.org/blogs/analysis/2017/07/claims-iran-violate-nuclear-accord; 'Don't repeat the Iraq War false WMD claims with Iran', IISS, 1 August 2017, https://www.iiss.org/blogs/analysis/2017/08/iran-war-false-

claims; 'The Iran nuclear deal is working – access debates are no cause for alarm', Survival Editors' Blog, 29 August 2017, https://www.iiss.org/blogs/survival-blog/2017/08/iran-nuclear-deal; 'Fixing an Iran nuclear deal that ain't broke', Survival Editors' Blog, 23 October 2017, https://www.iiss.org/blogs/survival-blog/2017/10/fixing-nuclear-deal; 'Trust in the IAEA's verification of Iran's nuclear activities', IISS, 5 December 2017, https://www.iiss.org/blogs/analysis/2017/12/iaea-verification; 'An Order of Priorities in Confronting Iran', *Survival: Global Politics and Strategy*, vol. 59, no. 2, April–May 2017, pp. 25–29; 'Critics are wrong: Iran remains in compliance with nuclear accord', Survival Editors' Blog, 15 June 2017, https://www.iiss.org/blogs/survival-blog/2017/06/iran-nuclear; 'Iran's Protests and the Fate of the Nuclear Deal', *Survival: Global Politics and Strategy*, vol. 60, no. 1, February–March 2018, pp. 69–74; Mark Fitzpatrick and Dana Allin, 'Iran nuclear deal on the ropes', Survival Editors' Blog, 1 May 2018, https://www.iiss.org/blogs/survival-blog/2018/05/iran-nuclear-deal; 'Pulling out of the Iran nuclear deal is Trump's most disastrous decision to date', *Prospect*, 9 May 2018, https://www.prospectmagazine.co.uk/world/pulling-out-of-the-iran-nuclear-deal-is-trumps-most-disastrous-decision-to-date; 'Pompeo's 12 angry demands won't restrain Iran', Survival Editors' Blog, 23 May 2018, https://www.iiss.org/blogs/survival-blog/2018/05/pompeos-12-demands.

2   Natural uranium ore contains 0.7% of the fissile isotope uranium 235. For use as fuel for power reactors, it needs to be enriched to 3.75–5% uranium 235. Research reactors require uranium fuel enriched to almost 20%. This percentage is the dividing line between LEU and HEU. Uranium enriched above 20% theoretically can be used for a nuclear weapon, but as a practical matter weapons need HEU at 80% or above, ideally at 93%.

3   'Israeli PM threatens to strike Iran', Al Jazeera, 17 July 2013, https://www.aljazeera.com/news/middleeast/2013/07/2013714214528446397.html.

4   The NPT neither prohibits nor explicitly allows the sensitive technologies of uranium enrichment and plutonium reprocessing. Some states believe that the right is provided for in Article IV.1 of the treaty, which states: 'Nothing in this Treaty shall be interpreted as affecting the inalienable right of all the Parties to the Treaty to develop research, production and use of nuclear energy for peaceful purposes without discrimination and in conformity with Articles I and II of this Treaty'. For the text of the treaty, see United Nations Office for Disarmament Affairs, 'Treaty on the Non-Proliferation of Nuclear Weapons (NPT)', https://www.un.org/disarmament/wmd/nuclear/npt/text.

5   Paul Richter and Ramin Mostaghim, 'Iran's Khamenei adds a twist to tough terms for nuclear talks', *Los Angeles Times*, 9 April 2015, http://www.latimes.com/world/middleeast/la-fg-iran-nuclear-khamenei-20150409-story.html#page=1.

6   'IRGC Deputy Commander: Inspection of Military Sites Impossible', Fars News Agency, 19 April 2015,

http://en.farsnews.com/newstext.aspx?nn=13940130000234.

7 'Iranian official: We'll allow "managed access" to military sites', *Times of Israel*, 24 May 2015, http://www.timesofisrael.com/iranian-official-well-allow-managed-access-to-military-sites/.

8 Office of US Senator Tom Cotton, 'Cotton and 46 Fellow Senators to Send Open Letter to the Leaders of the Islamic Republic of Iran', 9 March 2015, https://www.cotton.senate.gov/?p=press_release&id=120.

9 The full text of the deal is available on the European Parliament's website: 'Joint Comprehensive Plan of Action', 14 July 2015, http://www.europarl.europa.eu/delegations/en/d-ir/documents/eu-texts.

10 United States House of Representatives, Committee on Foreign Affairs, 'Iran nuclear agreement: The Administration's case, hearing before the Committee on Foreign Affairs, House of Representatives', 28 July 2015, https://www.gpo.gov/fdsys/pkg/CHRG-114hhrg95693/html/CHRG-114hhrg95693.htm. The figure is a matter of controversy and hard to pin down. President Trump often says the amount was US$150 billion, a figure typically used by conservative critics of the deal. The head of Iran's Central Bank put the amount at around US$30bn. See Jon Greenberg, 'Donald Trump says Iran got $150 billion and $1.8 billion in cash. That's Half True', Politifact, 27 April 2018, https://www.politifact.com/truth-o-meter/statements/2018/apr/27/donald-trump/donald-trump-iran-150-billion-and-18-billion-c.

11 Darius Dixon, 'Moniz: Test Results Back Up Assurances on Iran Deal', Politico, 22 July 2015, https://www.politico.com/story/2015/07/moniz-test-results-back-up-assurances-on-iran-deal-120507.

12 Calculating the breakout time is a mathematical exercise that depends on how many centrifuges are operated, their efficiency at enriching uranium and their configuration. It does not take into account motivation and other intangible factors.

13 JCPOA, Preface.

14 Even one of the European parties objected to extending the ban on Iranian missile testing imposed by UN Security Council Resolution 1929 (2010), on the basis that the ban had been included to pressure Iran to accept a deal limiting its nuclear programme, so there was no justification to continue such a ban if a nuclear deal could be made. See Philip Gordon, 'What's Wrong with Michael Flynn's Bluster on Iran? Plenty', *New York Times*, 2 February 2017, https://www.nytimes.com/2017/02/02/opinion/whats-wrong-with-michael-flynns-bluster-on-iran-plenty.html.

15 Testimony of then-Undersecretary of State for Political Affairs Wendy Sherman at a Senate Foreign Relations Committee Hearing on the Iran Nuclear Negotiations, 4 February 2014, http://www.shearman.com/~/media/Files/Services/Iran-Sanctions/US-Resources/Joint-Plan-of-Action/4-Feb-2014--Transcript-of-Senate-Foreign-Relations-Committee-Hearing-on-the-Iran-Nuclear-Negotiations-Panel-1.pdf.

16 JCPOA, Annex V.

17 JCPOA, paragraph 34.iv. Drawing the broader conclusion will require the absence of any lingering questions about Iran's intentions, and will likely take longer than eight years. Reaching this conclusion took seven years for Taiwan, and ten years for Turkey,

after each began to implement the Additional Protocol.

18 US National Intelligence Council, 'Iran: Nuclear Intentions and Capabilities', National Intelligence Estimate, November 2007, https://www.dni. gov/files/documents/Newsroom/ Press%20Releases/2007%20Press%20 Releases/20071203_release.pdf.

19 International Atomic Energy Agency, 'Implementation of the NPT Safeguards Agreement and relevant provisions of Security Council resolutions in the Islamic Republic of Iran: Report by the Director General', GOV/2011/65, 8 November 2011, https://www.iaea.org/ sites/default/files/gov2011-65.pdf.

20 IAEA, 'Implementation of the NPT Safeguards Agreement and relevant provisions of Security Council resolutions in the Islamic Republic of Iran: Report by the Director General', GOV/2015/34, 29 May 2015, paragraphs 65–68, https://www.iaea.org/sites/ default/files/gov-2015-34.pdf. Officials with whom the author discussed the report said it meant Iran had provided substantive answers to only one of the 12 areas of concern and partial answers to a second one.

21 For the text of the road map, see IAEA, 'Implementation of the NPT Safeguards Agreement and relevant provisions of Security Council resolutions in the Islamic Republic of Iran: Report by the Director General', GOV/2015/50, 27 August 2015, Annex II, p. 16, https://www.iaea.org/sites/ default/files/gov-2015-50-derestr.pdf.

22 JCPOA, Annex I, paragraph 66; Annex V, paragraph 9.

23 IAEA, 'Final Assessment on Past and Present Outstanding Issues regarding Iran's Nuclear Programme: Report by the Director General', GOV/2015/68, 2 December 2015, paragraph 62, https:// www.iaea.org/sites/default/files/gov- 2015-68.pdf.

24 Martin Malin, 'Five Takeaways from the IAEA's Report on Iran's Nuclear Past', Huffington Post, 7 December 2015, https://www.huffingtonpost. com/martin-malin-/iaea-iran-report- takeaways_b_8735838.html.

25 IAEA, 'Final Assessment on Past and Present Outstanding Issues regarding Iran's Nuclear Programme', paragraph 87.

26 Parisa Hafezi, 'Iran's Khamenei conditionally approves nuclear deal with powers', Reuters, 21 October 2015, https://www.reuters.com/article/ us-iran-nuclear-khamenei-idUSKC N0SF18720151021#p1wA4JTczuJdE pgk.97.

27 Arash Bahmani, 'How will Iran ratify the deal?', Al-Monitor, 5 August 2015, http://www.al-monitor.com/ pulse/originals/2015/08/irandeal- legal-path.html.

28 US Senate, Committee on Foreign Relations, 'Secretary Kerry's Remarks: SFRC Hearing on the Iran Nuclear Deal', 23 July 2015, https://www. foreign.senate.gov/imo/media/doc/07- 23-2015%20Secretary%20Kerry%20 Testimony.pdf.

29 See, for example, Isabel Kershner, 'Iran Deal Denounced by Netanyahu as "Historic Mistake"', New York Times, 14 July 2015, https://www.nytimes. com/2015/07/15/world/middleeast/ iran-nuclear-deal-israel.html.

30 'Transcript: President Obama's Full NPR Interview On Iran Nuclear Deal', National Public Radio, 7 April 2015, https://www.npr. org/2015/04/07/397933577/transcript- president-obamas-full-npr-interview- on-iran-nuclear-deal.

31 US Department of State, 'Daily Press Briefing – April 7, 2015', http://www.state. gov/r/pa/prs/dpb/2015/04/240401.htm.

32 'Critics Say U.S. Officials Promised "Anytime, Anywhere" Inspections In Iran Nuclear Deal', National Public Radio, 11 August 2015, https://www.npr.org/2015/08/11/431672987/critics-say-u-s-officials-promised-anytime-anywhere-inspections-in-iran-nuclear.

33 Fredrik Dahl, 'IAEA Now Has More Inspection Powers in Iran, Increased Knowledge of Its Nuclear Programme – Director General', International Atomic Energy Agency, 14 November 2017, https://www.iaea.org/newscenter/news/iaea-now-has-more-inspection-powers-in-iran-increased-knowledge-of-its-nuclear-programme-director-general.

34 IAEA, 'Final assessment on Past and Present Outstanding Issues regarding Iran's Nuclear Programme', paragraphs 53–57.

35 IAEA, 'Director General's Speech on Iran, the JCPOA and the IAEA', 14 November 2017, https://www.iaea.org/newscenter/statements/director-generals-speech-on-iran-the-jcpoa-and-the-iaea.

36 Author's communication with former senior official who was involved in the visits.

37 Jonathan Tirone and Ladane Nasseri, 'Iran Can Do More After Record Nuclear Inspections, IAEA Says', Bloomberg, 4 June 2018, https://www.bloomberg.com/news/articles/2018-06-04/iran-can-do-more-after-record-nuclear-inspections-iaea-says.

38 'Nuclear inspectors should have access to Iran military bases: Haley', Reuters, 25 August 2017, https://www.reuters.com/article/us-iran-nuclear-usa-haley/nuclear-inspectors-should-have-access-to-iran-military-bases-haley-idUSKCN1B524I.

39 Author's communication with Western government official.

40 IAEA, 'Director General's Speech on Iran'.

41 IAEA, 'Verification and monitoring in the Islamic Republic of Iran in light of United Nations Security Council resolution 2231 (2015); Report by the Director General', GOV/2017/24, 2 June 2017, paragraph 26, https://www.iaea.org/sites/default/files/gov2017-24.pdf.

42 David Albright and Olli Heinonen, 'Verifying Section T of the Iran Nuclear Deal: Iranian Military Site Access Essential to JCPOA Section T Verification', Institute for Science and International Security, 31 August 2017, http://isis-online.org/isis-reports/detail/verifying-section-t-of-the-iran-nuclear-deal.

43 Francois Murphy, 'IAEA chief calls for clarity on disputed section of Iran nuclear deal', Reuters, 26 September 2017, https://www.reuters.com/article/us-iran-nuclear-iaea/iaea-chief-calls-for-clarity-on-disputed-section-of-iran-nuclear-deal-idUSKCN1C12AN.

44 Joshua Block, 'What the IAEA doesn't know – or want to know – about Iran's nuclear program', The Hill, 18 October 2018, https://thehill.com/opinion/international/411734-what-the-iaea-doesnt-know-or-want-to-know-about-irans-nuclear-program.

45 Murphy, 'IAEA chief calls for clarity'.

46 Russian Federation Ministry of Foreign Affairs, 'Foreign Minister Sergey Lavrov's remarks and answers to media questions at the Moscow Nonproliferation Conference, October 20, 2017', 20 October 2017,

http://www.mid.ru/en/press_service/minister_speeches/-/asset_publisher/7OvQR5KJWVmR/content/id/2913751.

47 Eliott C. McLaughlin, 'Netanyahu says he has proof of secret Iranian nuclear program', CNN, 1 May 2018, https://www.cnn.com/2018/04/30/middleeast/netanyahu-iran-nuclear-program/index.html.

48 John Kerry, Twitter, 1 May 2018, https://twitter.com/johnkerry/status/991400032736825344.

49 White House, 'Statement by the Press Secretary on Israel's Announcement Related to Iranian Nuclear Weapons Development', 30 April 2018, https://www.whitehouse.gov/briefings-statements/statement-press-secretary-israels-announcement-related-iranian-nuclear-weapons-development.

50 Amir Tibon, 'In "Spelling Mistake," White House Says Iran Has a Nuclear Weapons Program', Haaretz, 1 May 2018, https://www.haaretz.com/middle-east-news/iran/in-spelling-mistake-white-house-says-iran-has-a-nuclear-program-1.6045782.

51 See, for example, John R. Bolton, 'How to Get Out of the Iran Nuclear Deal', National Review, 28 August 2017, https://www.nationalreview.com/2017/08/iran-nuclear-deal-exit-strategy-john-bolton-memo-trump/.

52 Richard Haass, Twitter, 1 May 2018, https://twitter.com/RichardHaass/status/991285070395727872.

53 JCPOA, Section T.

54 Robert Einhorn, 'Israeli intelligence coup could help Trump "fix" the Iran deal', Brookings, 4 May 2018, https://www.brookings.edu/blog/order-from-chaos/2018/05/04/israeli-intelligence-coup-could-help-trump-fix-the-iran-deal/.

55 William Tobey, 'Iran's Parchin Particles: Why Should Two Mites of Uranium Matter?', Foreign Policy, 7 July 2016, http://foreignpolicy.com/2016/07/07/irans-parchin-particles-why-should-two-mites-of-uranium-matter/.

56 IAEA, 'Final Assessment on Past and Present Outstanding Issues regarding Iran's Nuclear Programme', p. 11.

57 The quarterly reports are available on the IAEA's website: IAEA, 'IAEA and Iran – IAEA Reports', https://www.iaea.org/newscenter/focus/iran/iaea-and-iran-iaea-reports.

58 Chris Smith, 'Trump's Cold War with the C.I.A. Could Derail the Iran Deal', Vanity Fair, 6 October 2017, https://www.vanityfair.com/news/2017/10/trumps-cold-war-with-the-cia-could-derail-the-iran-deal.

59 John Hudson and Mark Seibel, 'Trump Keeps The Iran Deal In Place, While Threatening New Sanctions', Buzzfeed, 17 July 2017, https://www.buzzfeed.com/amphtml/markseibel/trump-certification-of-iran-nuclear-deal-comes-with-tough.

60 US Department of State, 'Department Press Briefing', 18 July 2017, https://www.state.gov/r/pa/prs/dpb/2017/07/272665.htm.

61 Nahal Toosi, 'Haley: Trump "has grounds" to say Iran violating nuclear deal', Politico, 5 September 2017, https://www.politico.com/story/2017/09/05/trump-iran-violate-nuclear-deal-nikki-haley-242331.

62 Office of US Senator Tom Cotton, 'Cotton and Colleagues Urge Tillerson Not to Certify Iran Compliance with the JCPOA', 11 July 2017, https://www.cotton.senate.gov/?p=press_release&id=744.

63 Author communications with officials involved.

64 JCPOA, Annex I, C.14.

65 Author communication with a former US State Department official.

66 Germany Federal Ministry of the Interior, '2016 Annual Report on the Protection of the Constitution (Facts and Trends)', June 2017, https://www.verfassungsschutz.de/embed/annual-report-2016-summary.pdf.

67 David Albright and Andrea Stricker, 'Analysis of the IAEA's Sixth Iran Nuclear Deal Report: A Return to More Limited Data', Institute for Science and International Security, 5 June 2017, http://isis-online.org/isis-reports/detail/analysis-of-the-iaeas-sixth-iran-nuclear-deal-report-a-return-to-more-limit.

68 David Albright and Andrea Stricker, 'JCPOA Exemptions Revealed', Institute for Science and International Security, 1 September 2016, http://isis-online.org/isis-reports/detail/jcpoa-exemptions-revealed.

69 Mahsa Rouhi, 'Trump Should Avoid Believing the Myths of the JCPOA', National Interest, 21 November 2017, http://nationalinterest.org/feature/trump-should-avoid-believing-the-myths-the-jcpoa-23312.

70 International Crisis Group, 'The Illogic of the U.S. Sanctions Snapback on Iran', 2 November 2018, https://d2071andvipowj.cloudfront.net/B064-the-illogic-of-the-us-sanctions-snapback-on-iran.pdf.

71 US Senate, Committee on Armed Services, 'Hearing to Receive Testimony on Worldwide Threats', 23 May 2017, p. 59, https://www.armed-services.senate.gov/imo/media/doc/17-49_05-23-17.pdf.

72 White House, 'Remarks by President Obama in Press Conference after GCC Summit', 14 May 2015, https://obamawhitehouse.archives.gov/the-press-office/2015/05/14/remarks-president-obama-press-conference-after-gcc-summit.

73 US Department of State, 'After the Deal: A New Iran Strategy – Remarks, Mike Pompeo', 21 May 2018, https://www.state.gov/secretary/remarks/2018/05/282301.htm.

74 H.R. 1191 – Iran Nuclear Agreement Review Act of 2015, Public Law 114–17, 22 May 2015, https://www.congress.gov/bill/114th-congress/house-bill/1191/text.

75 White House, 'Remarks by President Trump on Iran Strategy', 13 October 2017, https://www.whitehouse.gov/briefings-statements/remarks-president-trump-iran-strategy.

76 White House, 'Statement by the President on the Iran Nuclear Deal', 12 January 2018, https://www.whitehouse.gov/briefings-statements/statement-president-iran-nuclear-deal/.

77 Interviews with officials involved.

78 Ben Smith, 'Macron Says Trump Will Likely Kill The Iran Deal', BuzzFeed News, 25 April 2018, https://www.buzzfeed.com/bensmith/macron-says-trump-will-likely-kill-the-iran-deal?utm_term=.na39V4VOr#.rlvGDoD8b.

79 Madeline Conway, 'Bolton calls regime change the "only long-term solution" in Iran', Politico, 17 November 2016, https://www.politico.com/story/2016/11/john-bolton-iran-regime-change-231586.

80 Bolton, 'How to Get Out of the Iran Nuclear Deal'.

81 John R. Bolton, 'To Stop Iran's Bomb, Bomb Iran', New York Times, 26 March 2015, https://www.nytimes.com/2015/03/26/opinion/to-stop-irans-bomb-bomb-iran.html?_r=0.

82 'Rep. Mike Pompeo: One year later, Obama's Iran nuclear deal puts us at increased risk', Fox News, 14 July 2016, http://www.foxnews.com/opinion/2016/07/14/rep-mike-pompeo-one-year-later-obama-s-iran-nuclear-deal-puts-us-at-increased-risk.html.

83 Jake Sullivan, 'Trump's Only Iran Strategy Is to Punish Iran', *Atlantic*, 19 May 2018, https://www.theatlantic.com/international/archive/2018/05/trump-iran-jcpoa/560759/.

84 US Department of State, 'Background Briefing on President Trump's Decision To Withdraw From the JCPOA', 8 May 2018, https://www.state.gov/r/pa/prs/ps/2018/05/281959.htm.

85 'New U.S. envoy warns German firms to wind down business in Iran', Reuters, 8 May 2018, https://www.reuters.com/article/us-iran-nuclear-germany-grenell/new-us-envoy-warns-german-firms-to-wind-down-business-in-iran-idUSKBN1I92YP.

86 Michael Birnbaum, 'E.U. leader lights into Trump: "With friends like that, who needs enemies?"', *Washington Post*, 16 May 2018, https://www.washingtonpost.com/news/worldviews/wp/2018/05/16/e-u-leader-lights-into-trump-with-friends-like-that-who-needs-enemies/?utm_term=.5b4e8f7cb4e4.

87 International Crisis Group, 'The Iran Nuclear Deal at Two: A Status Report', 16 January 2018, p. 10, https://www.crisisgroup.org/middle-east-north-africa/gulf-and-arabian-peninsula/iran/181-iran-nuclear-deal-two-status-report.

88 US Department of State, 'After the Deal: A New Iran Strategy'.

89 See, for example, Richard Goldberg and Jamie Fly, 'What Washington can do to support Iran's protesters', *New York Post*, 2 January 2018, https://nypost.com/2018/01/02/what-washington-can-do-to-support-irans-protesters/.

90 In an interview on 3 January 2018, for example, Vice President Mike Pence said 'my hope is that the people who are taking to the streets in Iran know that under President Donald Trump they are not alone'. See Peter Heinlein, 'VP Pence Vows US Solidarity With Iranian Protesters', Voice of America, 3 January 2018, https://www.voanews.com/a/vice-president-mike-pence-iran-interview/4191033.html.

91 Barbara Slavin, 'Latest Iran poll suggests Trump rhetoric benefits hardliners', Al-Monitor, 2 February 2018, http://www.al-monitor.com/pulse/originals/2018/02/iran-poll-suggests-trump-rhetoric-benefiting-hardliners.html#ixzz55zXhegpW.

92 Nancy Gallagher, Ebrahim Mohseni and Clay Ramsay, 'The Ramifications of Rouhani's Re-election – The Questionnaire', Center for International and Security Studies at Maryland, July 2017, http://www.cissm.umd.edu/publications/ramifications-rouhanis-re-election-questionnaire.

93 Paulina Izewicz, 'Iran deal decertification looms: what's next?', IISS, 12 October 2017, https://www.iiss.org/blogs/analysis/2017/10/iran-deal-decertification-looms.

94 European Union External Action Service, 'Iran Deal: EU and partners set up mechanism to protect legitimate business with Iran', 25 September 2018, https://eeas.europa.eu/headquarters/headquarters-homepage/51066/iran-deal-eu-and-partners-set-mechanism-protect-legitimate-business-iran_en.

95 European External Action Service, 'Joint statement by High Representative Federica Mogherini

and Foreign Ministers Jean-Yves Le Drian, Heiko Maas and Jeremy Hunt, and Finance Ministers Bruno Le Maire, Olaf Scholz and Philip Hammond', 2 November 2018, https://eeas.europa.eu/headquarters/headquarters-homepage/53230/joint-statement-high-representative-federica-mogherini-and-foreign-ministers-jean-yves-le_en.

[96] Saeed Kamali Dehghan and Julian Borger, 'Iran threatens to withdraw from nuclear weapons treaty', *Guardian*, 24 April 2018, https://www.theguardian.com/world/2018/apr/24/iran-threatens-to-withdraw-from-nuclear-weapons-treaty-npt.

[97] IAEA, 'Director General's Speech on Iran'.

Chapter Two

[1] This chapter draws on a report by the author previously published by the IISS: see Paulina Izewicz, 'Assessing the JCPOA Procurement Channel', IISS, 29 March 2018, https://www.iiss.org/blogs/analysis/2018/03/jcpoa-procurement-channel.

[2] Ariana Rowberry, 'Sixty Years of "Atoms for Peace" and Iran's Nuclear Program', Brookings Institution, 18 December 2013, https://www.brookings.edu/blog/up-front/2013/12/18/sixty-years-of-atoms-for-peace-and-irans-nuclear-program/.

[3] For more on the network of A.Q. Khan, see IISS, *Nuclear Black Markets: Pakistan, A.Q. Khan and the rise of proliferation networks – a net assessment* (London: IISS, 2007).

[4] Resolutions 1696 (2006); 1737 (2006); 1747 (2007); 1803 (2008); 1835 (2008); 1929 (2010).

[5] See United Nations Security Council, 'Final report of the Panel of Experts established pursuant to resolution 1929 (2010)', S/2013/331, 5 June 2013, http://undocs.org/S/2013/331; UN Security Council, 'Final report of the Panel of Experts established pursuant to resolution 1929 (2010)',

S/2014/394, 11 June 2014, http://undocs.org/S/2014/394.

[6] Ian J. Stewart and Nick Gillard, 'Iran's illicit procurement activities: Past, present and future', Project Alpha, 24 July 2015, p. 13, http://projectalpha.eu/wp-content/uploads/sites/21/2015/07/20150724_-_Iran_Illicit_trade_past_present_future_FINAL.pdf.

[7] *Ibid.* Note that these cases involve known procurements; unknown attempts may well paint a different picture. Similarly, it is possible that Germany, the United Kingdom and the United States are more likely to detect export control violations, thus skewing the dataset.

[8] See 'Joint Comprehensive Plan of Action', 14 July 2015, Annex IV, paragraph 6, http://www.europarl.europa.eu/delegations/en/d-ir/documents/eu-texts; United Nations Security Council, 'Resolution 2231 (2015)', S/RES/2231, 20 July 2015, Annex B, paragraph 2, https://undocs.org/S/RES/2231(2015).

[9] UN Security Council, 'Resolution 2231 (2015): Nuclear-related transfers and activities (procurement channel)', http://www.un.org/en/sc/2231/restrictions-

nuclear.shtml. The documents referred to are periodically updated, and are available, in their latest iteration, on the website of the Nuclear Suppliers Group: http://www.nuclearsuppliersgroup. org/en/guidelines.

10 UN Security Council, 'Final report of the Panel of Experts established pursuant to resolution 1929 (2010)', S/2014/394, pp. 3–4.

11 For comparison, according to statistics for 2015 published by the UK's national licensing body, the Export Control Organisation, 70% of applications for exports that required a licence were processed within 20 working days, and 99% within 60; median processing times ranged between 12 and 21 days. See UK Foreign & Commonwealth Office, 'UK Annual Report on Strategic Export Controls 2015', 21 July 2016, p. 18, https://assets.publishing.service. gov.uk/government/uploads/system/ uploads/attachment_data/file/539753/ UK_Annual_Report_on_Strategic_ Export_Controls_2015.pdf.

12 The UN Security Council has made a model end-user certification available, along with detailed explanations: UN Security Council, 'Resolution 2231 (2015): Nuclear-related transfers and activities (procurement channel)'.

13 UN Security Council, 'Implementation of Security Council resolution 2231(2015): Fifth report of the Secretary-General', S/2018/602, 12 June 2018, paragraph 16, http://undocs. org/S/2018/602.

14 David Albright and Andrea Stricker, 'Previously Sanctioned Iranian Entities Doing Business in China', Institute for Science and International Security, 7 July 2016, p. 3, http:// isis-online.org/uploads/isis-reports/ documents/Previously_Sanctioned_

Iranian_Entities_Doing_Business_ in_China_7Jul2016_Final.pdf. Author communications with officials involved confirmed the firm in question was Austrian.

15 Ali Kushki, 'Missing "political will" in UK obstacle to yellow cake deal', Tehran Times, 17 April 2017, http:// www.tehrantimes.com/news/412696/ Missing-political-will-in-UK-obstacle-to-yellow-cake-deal.

16 Germany is understood to be the most active state in the Procurement Channel.

17 The IAEA, which can participate in the PWG as an observer if the goods under consideration are destined for nuclear applications, has done so on two occasions. At least one application for such end use is known to have been approved.

18 UN Security Council, 'Fifth six-month report of the Facilitator on the implementation of Security Council resolution 2231 (2015)', S/2018/624, 21 June 2018, paragraph 24, http://undocs. org/S/2018/624.

19 Albright and Stricker, 'Previously Sanctioned Iranian Entities Doing Business in China', p. 2.

20 UK Department for International Trade, 'The procurement channel for export of nuclear and dual-use goods and services to Iran: Guidance for UK exporters', June 2017, https:// assets.publishing.service.gov.uk/ government/uploads/system/uploads/ attachment_data/file/652965/17-procurement-channel-guidance.pdf.

21 UN Security Council, 'Resolution 2231 (2015): Nuclear-related transfers and activities (procurement channel)'.

22 UN Security Council, 'Fifth six-month report of the Facilitator on the implementation of Security Council

resolution 2231 (2015)', S/2018/624, paragraph 33.

23 See, for example, Ian J. Stewart and Nick Gillard, 'Sabotage? Iranian exhibition gives insights into illicit procurement methods and challenges', Project Alpha, 8 September 2014, http://kcl-digi-prod-wa-wordp-ne-04. azurewebsites.net/alpha/wp-content/ uploads/sites/21/2014/11/20140908-_ Project_Alpha_-_Sabotage_amended. pdf; Stewart and Gillard, 'Iran's illicit procurement activities: Past, present and future'.

24 'Czech Parliament Rejects Lifting Nuclear Ban Against Iran', Radio Farda, 10 September 2017, https:// en.radiofarda.com/a/czech-parliament-uphold-law-banning-nuclear-supplies-to-iran/28726183. html; Chris Johnstone, 'Czech Parliament Votes to Overturn Ban on Deliveries to Iran Nuclear Plant', Radio Prague, 19 April 2018, https:// www.radio.cz/en/section/news/czech-parliament-votes-to-overturn-ban-on-deliveries-to-iran-nuclear-plant.

25 UN Security Council, 'Final report of the Panel of Experts established pursuant to resolution 1929 (2010)', S/2014/394, paragraphs 65–66.

26 UN Security Council, 'Final report of the Panel of Experts established pursuant to resolution 1929 (2010)', S/2015/401, 2 June 2015, paragraphs 38–39, http://undocs.org/S/2015/401.

27 Germany Federal Ministry of the Interior, '2015 Annual Report on the Protection of the Constitution (Facts and Trends)', June 2016, p. 30, https:// www.verfassungsschutz.de/en/public-relations/publications/annual-reports/ annual-report-2015-summary.

28 Germany Federal Ministry of the Interior, '2016 Annual Report on the Protection of the Constitution (Facts and Trends)', June 2017, p. 33, https:// www.verfassungsschutz.de/en/public-relations/publications/annual-reports/ annual-report-2016-summary.

29 Benjamin Weinthal, 'Iran Still on the Hunt for Nuclear Weapons Technology Across Germany', *Weekly Standard*, 7 July 2017, http://www.weeklystandard. com/iran-still-on-the-hunt-for-nuclear-weapons-technology-across-germany/ article/2008747.

30 UN Security Council, 'Fourth report of the Secretary-General on the implementation of Security Council resolution 2231 (2015)', S/2017/1030, 8 December 2017, paragraphs 7, 19, https://undocs.org/S/2017/1030.

31 UN Security Council, 'Fifth report of the Secretary-General on the implementation of Security Council resolution 2231 (2015)', S/2018/602, paragraph 18.

32 UN Security Council, 'Third report of the Secretary-General on the implementation of Security Council resolution 2231 (2015)', S/2017/515, 20 June 2017, paragraph 23, https:// undocs.org/S/2017/515.

33 See, for example, Germany Federal Ministry of the Interior, '2016 Annual Report on the Protection of the Constitution (Facts and Trends)', p. 33.

34 JCPOA, Annex IV, paragraph 6.6.

35 UN Security Council, 'Resolution 2231 (2015)', S/RES/2231, Annex B, paragraph 6.c.

36 David Albright and Andrea Stricker, 'The Iran Nuclear Deal's Procurement Channel: Overcoming Post-Implementation Day Issues', Institute for Science and International Security, 21 April 2016, p. 9, http://isis-online. org/uploads/isis-reports/documents/ JCPOA_Procurement_Channel_Post_

Implementation_Day_21April2016_
Final1_1.pdf.

37 UN Security Council, 'Fifth report
of the Secretary-General on the
implementation of Security Council
resolution 2231 (2015)', S/2018/602,
paragraph 20.

38 See David Albright and Andrea
Stricker, 'Iranian Atomic Energy
Organization Attempted Carbon
Fiber Procurement', Institute for
Science and International Security,
7 July 2016, http://isis-online.org/
uploads/isis-reports/documents/
AEOI_Attempted_Carbon_Fiber_
Procurement_7Jul2016.pdf.

Chapter Three

1 This chapter draws on a report by
two of the authors: Michael Elleman
and Mark Fitzpatrick, 'Are Iran's
ballistic missiles designed to be
nuclear capable?', IISS, 28 February
2018, https://www.iiss.org/blogs/
analysis/2018/02/iran-missiles-nuclear-
capable. This report was supported by
a grant from the John D. and Catherine
T. MacArthur Foundation.

2 White House Press Office, 'Statement
by the President on the Iran Nuclear
Deal', 12 January 2018, https://www.
whitehouse.gov/briefings-statements/
statement-president-iran-nuclear-deal/.

3 United Nations Security Council,
'Resolution 2231 (2015)', S/RES/2231,
20 July 2015, Annex B, paragraph 3,
https://undocs.org/S/RES/2231(2015).

4 Greg Thielmann, 'The Iranian Ballistic
Missile Launches That Didn't Happen',
LobeLog, 16 March 2016, http://
lobelog.com/the-iranian-ballistic-
missile-launches-that-didnt-happen/.

5 The United States, for its part, has
adopted a definition of a nuclear
weapon as 'any weapon that contains
or uses nuclear material'. Nuclear
material is further defined as 'material
containing any – (A) plutonium; (B)
uranium not in the form of ore or
ore residue that contains the mixture
of isotopes as occurring in nature;
(C) enriched uranium, defined as
uranium that contains the isotope 233
or 235 or both in such amount that the
abundance ratio of the sum of those
isotopes to the isotope 238 is greater
than the ratio of the isotope 235 or the
isotope 238 occurring in nature; or (D)
uranium 233'. See U.S. Code Title 18,
Part I, Chapter 39, paragraphs 831–32,
available at https://www.law.cornell.
edu/uscode/text/18/part-I/chapter-39.

6 Louis Charbonneau, 'Exclusive:
Iran missile tests were "in defiance
of" U.N. resolution – U.S., allies',
Reuters, 29 March 2016, https://www.
reuters.com/article/us-iran-missiles/
exclusive-iran-missile-tests-were-in-
defiance-of-u-n-resolution-u-s-allies-
idUSKCN0WV2HE.

7 United Nations Security Council,
'Third report of the Secretary-General
on the implementation of Security
Council resolution 2231 (2015)',
S/2017/515, 20 June 2017, paragraph 3,
https://undocs.org/S/2017/515.

8 UN Security Council, 'Fourth report
of the Secretary-General on the
implementation of Security Council
resolution 2231 (2015)', S/2017/1030, 8
December 2017, paragraph 21, https://
undocs.org/S/2017/1030.

9   *Ibid.*, paragraph 23.

10 Aaron Karp, 'Missile Technology Control Regime: Stemming the Spread of Missiles: Hits, Misses, and Hard Cases', Arms Control Association, 13 April 2012, https://www.armscontrol.org/taxonomy/term/49?page=2.

11 Richard Speier, 'The Missile Technology Control Regime: Case Study of a Multilateral Negotiation', unpublished manuscript, submitted to the United States Institute of Peace under grant SG-31-95, Washington DC, November 1995, p. 22.

12 The US also had more sophisticated nuclear weapons that weighed considerably less than 500 kg: the W54 warhead used for the *Davy Crockett* recoilless-spigot gun in the 1950s weighed about 23 kg.

13 Although the Soviet Union argued that the *Scud*-B had a range of 299 km, and therefore was not a Category I system, the 1,000 kg mass of the *Scud*-B's warhead put the system well over the threshold. As Iraq demonstrated in the late 1980s and early 1990s, a warhead can sacrifice some mass for greater range.

14 Interview with a former member of the UN Panel of Experts created pursuant to resolution 1929 (2010), January 2018.

15 'Missile Technology Control Regime (MTCR) Annex Handbook 2017', pp. iii and 329–39, http://mtcr.info/wordpress/wp-content/uploads/2017/10/MTCR-Handbook-2017-INDEXED-FINAL-Digital.pdf.

16 White House Press Office, 'Statement of Interdiction Principles: Fact Sheet', 4 September 2003, https://www.state.gov/t/isn/c27726.htm.

17 See, for example, Peter Van Ham, 'The MTCR at 30: Ideas to Strengthen the Missile Technology Control Norm', Cligendael, November 2017, https://www.clingendael.org/sites/default/files/2017-11/PB_The_MCTR_at_30.pdf.

18 Nick Wadhams and Kambiz Foroohar, 'Haley Says Missile Parts Prove Iran Violated UN Resolutions', Bloomberg, 14 December 2017, https://www.bloomberg.com/news/articles/2017-12-14/haley-says-missile-parts-prove-iran-is-violating-un-resolutions-jb6u2ik9. Haley additionally claimed, without legal basis, that the missile transfer was also a violation of the JCPOA.

19 Rick Gladstone, 'Iran Violated Yemen Arms Embargo, U.N. Experts Say', *New York Times*, 12 January 2018, https://www.nytimes.com/2018/01/12/world/middleeast/iran-yemen-saudi-arabia-arms-embargo-un.html.

20 Israel's presumably nuclear-armed missiles are the most lethal among the states normally considered to comprise the Middle East. Israel's *Jericho*-III intermediate-range ballistic missile may have the longest range, reportedly of 5,000 km. Saudi Arabia's *Dongfeng*-3 missiles imported from China in 1987 have a 4,000 km range, although the missiles have never been test-launched in Saudi Arabia and their operational capability is uncertain.

21 United States Senate, Committee on Banking, Housing, and Urban Affairs, 'Statement of Mr. Michael Elleman – Iran's Ballistic Missile Program – Before the U.S. Senate Committee on Banking, Housing, and Urban Affairs', 24 May 2016, https://www.banking.senate.gov/imo/media/doc/052416_Elleman Testimony.pdf.

22 Max Fisher, 'Deep in the Desert, Iran Quietly Advances Missile Technology', *New York Times*, 23 May 2018, https://

www.nytimes.com/2018/05/23/world/
middleeast/iran-missiles.html.

[23] Jeremy Binnie and Nick Hansen, 'Iran Releases *Khorramshahr* Missile Test Video', *Jane's Defence Weekly*, 28 September 2017, http://www.janes. com/article/74455/iran-releases-khorramshahr-missile-test-video.

[24] US Department of the Treasury, 'Treasury Sanctions Those Involved in Ballistic Missile Procurement for Iran', 17 January 2016, https://www.treasury. gov/press-center/press-releases/Pages/jl0322.aspx.

[25] IISS, *Iran's Ballistic Missile Capabilities: A Net Assessment* (IISS: London, 2010), p. 122.

[26] 'Iran warns Israel of military deterrence, missile might', Al-Alam, 25 May 2014, http://en.alalam.ir/news/1597338; 'Iran's statement in response to Trump's speech, US new policy', Islamic Republic News Agency, 13 October 2017, http://www. irna.ir/en/News/82694750.

[27] William J. Broad and David E. Sanger, 'Relying on Computer, U.S. Seeks to Prove Iran's Nuclear Aims', *New York Times*, 13 November 2005, http://www. nytimes.com/2005/11/13/international/middleeast/13nukes.html.

[28] An altitude of 600 m is also reasonably consistent with the dispersal of chemical bomblets containing mustard gas or an equivalently toxic chemical agent. The altitude is probably too low for sarin, Tabun or VX, all of which possess a large enough toxicity to cover a much larger territory. Conventional, high-explosive cluster warheads are typically dispersed at much lower altitudes.

[29] Michael Adler, 'US Briefs on Alleged Iranian Nuclear Warhead Work', Agence France-Presse, 10 October 2005; Dafna Linzer, 'Strong Leads and Dead Ends in Nuclear Case Against Iran', *Washington Post*, 8 February 2006, http://www. washingtonpost.com/wp-dyn/content/article/2006/02/07/AR2006020702126. html.

[30] Mark Fitzpatrick, 'Assessing Iran's Nuclear Programme', *Survival: Global Politics and Strategy*, vol. 48, no. 3, Autumn 2006, pp. 5–26 (p. 10).

[31] International Atomic Energy Agency, 'Implementation of the NPT Safeguards Agreement and Relevant Provisions of Security Council Resolutions 1737 (2006), 1747 (2007), 1803 (2008) and 1835 (2008) in the Islamic Republic of Iran', GOV/2010/10, 18 February 2010, paragraph 41, https://www.iaea.org/sites/default/files/gov2010-10.pdf.

[32] The total volume of the weapons bay in the *Ghadr*-1 re-entry vehicle is about 0.33 cubic metres. When loaded with a conventional high explosive, this translates to a weapons mass of about 600 kg. The structural components of the re-entry vehicle probably weigh 150–300 kg, depending on the reinforcements required. The Soviet-made *Scud*-B, for example, has a total warhead mass of 987 kg, of which 799 kg is high-explosive material, and 188 kg is inert shell, with fuses and other accessories.

[33] Jeremy Binnie and Andy Dinville, 'Satellite imagery shows accuracy of Iran's ballistic missiles', *Jane's Defence Weekly*, 31 October 2012.

[34] Behnam Ben Taleblu, 'Iranian Ballistic Missile Tests Since the Nuclear Deal – 2.0', Foundation for Defense of Democracies, 25 January 2018, http://www.defenddemocracy.org/content/uploads/documents/MEMO_IranBallisticMissile.pdf.

35 'Photos Show IRGC Used *Zolfaqar*, *Qiam* Missiles in Deir Ezzur Attacks', Fars News Agency, 19 June 2017, http://en.farsnews.com/newstext.aspx?nn=13960329000502.

36 Alireza Nader, 'Profile: Revolutionary Guards Chief Gen. Jafari', The Iran Primer, United States Institute of Peace, 21 January 2013, http://iranprimer.usip.org/blog/2013/jan/21/profile-revolutionary-guards-chief-gen-jafari.

37 'Iran says UN resolution not linked to ballistic missiles', Agence France-Press, 20 July 2015, https://www.yahoo.com/news/iran-says-un-resolution-not-linked-ballistic-missiles-175508977.html?ref=gs.

38 Javad Zarif, 'Iranian Foreign Minister: "Arab Affairs Are Iran's Business"', *Atlantic*, 9 October 2017, https://www.theatlantic.com/international/archive/2017/10/iran-persian-gulf-jcpoa/542421/.

39 Javad Zarif, 'We Do Not Have a Nuclear Weapons Program', *New York Times*, 6 April 2006, http://www.nytimes.com/2006/04/06/opinion/we-do-not-have-a-nuclear-weapons-program.html.

40 Ahmad Majidyar, 'I.R.G.C.: No Need to Boost Our Missile Range as They Reach Most U.S. Bases in Mideast', Middle East Institute, 31 October 2017, http://www.mei.edu/content/io/irgc-no-need-boost-our-missile-range-they-reach-most-us-bases-mideast.

41 Bozorgmehr Sharafedin, 'Iran warns it would increase missile range if threatened by Europe', Reuters, 26 November 2017, https://www.reuters.com/article/us-iran-missiles-europe/iran-warns-it-would-increase-missile-range-if-threatened-by-europe-idUSKBN1DQ007.

42 Michael Elleman, 'Banning Long-Range Missiles in the Middle East: A First Step for Regional Arms Control', *Arms Control Today*, 2 May 2012, https://www.armscontrol.org/act/2012_05/Banning_Long-Range_Missiles_In_the_Middle_East_A_First_Step_For_Regional_Arms_Control.

43 US National Air and Space Intelligence Center, 'Ballistic and Cruise Missile Threat', June 2017, p. 2, http://www.nasic.af.mil/Portals/19/images/Fact%20Sheet%20Images/2017%20Ballistic%20and%20Cruise%20Missile%20Threat_Final_small.pdf?ver=2017-07-21-083234-343.

44 Bill Gertz, 'Iran Conducts Space Launch: Simorgh launcher part of long range missile program', *Washington Free Beacon*, 20 April 2016, https://freebeacon.com/national-security/iran-conducts-space-launch; Lucas Tomlinson, 'Iran rocket suffered "catastrophic failure," likely blew up, US official says', Fox News, 28 July 2017, http://www.foxnews.com/world/2017/07/28/iran-rocket-suffered-catastrophic-failure-likely-blew-up-us-official-says.html.

45 Richard Goldberg and Behnam Ben Taleblu, 'Iran's New Missile Cap Offer Is a Total Sham', *National Interest*, 8 November 2017, http://nationalinterest.org/feature/irans-new-missile-cap-offer-sham-23108.

46 'Photos Show IRGC Used *Zolfaqar*, *Qiam* Missiles in Deir Ezzur Attacks', Fars News Agency.

47 Based on author interviews with Russian specialists, including Dr Vadim Vorobei, who was hired by Iran in the late 1990s to provide lectures on missile-manufacturing technologies.

48 'Iran tests new missile after U.S. criticizes arms program', Reuters, 23 September 2017, https://www.

reuters.com/article/us-iran-military-missiles/iran-tests-new-missile-after-u-s-criticizes-arms-program-idUSKCN1BY07B.

49 Ali Arouzi, 'Iran Shows Off *Khorramshahr* Ballistic Missile After Trump Speech', NBC News, 22 September 2017, https://www.nbcnews.com/news/world/iran-shows-khorramshahr-ballistic-missile-after-trump-speech-n803701.

Conclusions

1 Bethan McKernan, 'Iran's supreme leader lists demands for staying in nuclear deal', *Independent*, 24 May 2018, https://www.independent.co.uk/news/world/middle-east/iran-nuclear-deal-latest-ayatollah-ali-khamenei-us-sanctions-donald-trump-mike-pompeo-a8367096.html.

2 Julian Pecquet, 'US stands alone on Iran at Security Council', Al-Monitor, 26 September 2018, https://www.al-monitor.com/pulse/originals/2018/09/un-security-council-trump-iran-nuclear-deal.html.

3 Bill Faries, 'Iran's Zarif Tells Trump to "Try Respect" Instead of Threats, Sanctions', Bloomberg, 31 July 2018, https://www.bloomberg.com/news/articles/2018-07-31/zarif-tells-trump-to-try-respect-instead-of-threats-sanctions.

INDEX

⌢IISS ADELPHI BOOKS

ADELPHI 464–465

Once and Future Partners:
The United States, Russia and
Nuclear Non-proliferation

eds William C. Potter and
Sarah Bidgood

ISBN 978-1-138-36636-7

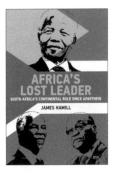

ADELPHI 463

Africa's Lost Leader:
South Africa's continental role
since apartheid

James Hamill

ISBN 978-1-138-54965-4

ADELPHI 462

**Renewing America's
Nuclear Arsenal:**
Options for the 21st Century

James E. Doyle

ISBN 978-0-8153-8466-3

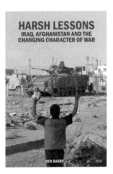

ADELPHI 461

Harsh Lessons: Iraq, Afghanistan
and the changing character
of war

Ben Barry

ISBN 978-1-138-06096-8

For credit card orders call **+44 (0) 1264 343 071**
or e-mail **book.orders@tandf.co.uk**
Orders can also be placed at **www.iiss.org**

Routledge
Taylor & Francis Group

Adelphi books are published eight times a year by Routledge Journals, an imprint of Taylor & Francis, 4 Park Square, Milton Park, Abingdon, Oxfordshire OX14 4RN, UK.

A subscription to the institution print edition, ISSN 1944-5571, includes free access for any number of concurrent users across a local area network to the online edition, ISSN 1944-558X. Taylor & Francis has a flexible approach to subscriptions enabling us to match individual libraries' requirements. This journal is available via a traditional institutional subscription (either print with free online access, or online-only at a discount) or as part of our libraries, subject collections or archives. For more information on our sales packages please visit www.tandfonline.com/page/librarians.

2018 Annual Adelphi Subscription Rates			
Institution	£719	US$1,262	€1,063
Individual	£254	US$434	€347
Online only	£629	US$1,104	€930

Dollar rates apply to subscribers outside Europe. Euro rates apply to all subscribers in Europe except the UK and the Republic of Ireland where the pound sterling price applies. All subscriptions are payable in advance and all rates include postage. Journals are sent by air to the USA, Canada, Mexico, India, Japan and Australasia. Subscriptions are entered on an annual basis, i.e. January to December. Payment may be made by sterling cheque, dollar cheque, international money order, National Giro, or credit card (Amex, Visa, Mastercard).

For a complete and up-to-date guide to Taylor & Francis journals and books publishing programmes, and details of advertising in our journals, visit our website: **http://www.tandfonline.com.**

Ordering information:
USA/Canada: Taylor & Francis Inc., Journals Department, 530 Walnut Street, Suite 850, Philadelphia, PA 19106, USA. **UK/Europe/Rest of World:** Routledge Journals, T&F Customer Services, T&F Informa UK Ltd., Sheepen Place, Colchester, Essex, CO3 3LP, UK.

Advertising enquiries to:
USA/Canada: The Advertising Manager, Taylor & Francis Inc., 530 Walnut Street, Suite 850, Philadelphia, PA 19106, USA. Tel: +1 (800) 354 1420. Fax: +1 (215) 207 0050. **UK/Europe/Rest of World**: The Advertising Manager, Routledge Journals, Taylor & Francis, 4 Park Square, Milton Park, Abingdon, Oxfordshire OX14 4RN, UK. Tel: +44 (0) 20 7017 6000. Fax: +44 (0) 20 7017 6336.